# CONT

# JOHN McGRATH

# POLICE

# RECRUITMENT GUIDE

Published by Digital Dream Publishing 2015

ISBN-13: 978-1517221379
ISBN-10: 1517221374

# INTRODUCTION

Becoming a police officer is still something many people aspire to. It is a very rewarding and at times exciting career that opens up a wealth of progression opportunities. Some of those that apply may have been a Special Constable or PCSO first, gaining valuable experience and a thirst to become a regular police officer. The numbers of police officers have dropped and recruitment frozen or reduced. However, most forces are in need of new recruits to replace those retiring or leaving the job. It is a job that is certainly challenging in these times of austerity. Many thousands apply to become police officers, but of these only around 5% secure a position. If you fail any part of the process you have to wait a minimum of six months before you can apply again.

With roughly 1 in 10 police constable applicants making it to a job offer. Around 70% of those, fail the application form Competency Based Questions (CBQ). These questions are designed to show you meet the necessary skills required of a police officer using the Skills for Justice Policing Professional Framework. Understand how to weave key words into a strong example for each of the four questions, whilst still telling a short story. Your chances of passing this first hurdle and getting invited to an assessment centre are greatly increased.

Those that go onto the assessment centre also limit their chances, either through not understanding the process or simply through lack of preparation. With a pass grade of 60% for the majority of forces and over half of the marks required to pass coming from the role play element followed by a third from two written exercises.

This book uses the latest core competencies and changes to the assessment centre from August 2015. It has plenty of hints and

tips from both examiners and successful applicants to keep it up to date and relevant and reflect the latest process. I could have written a book with every last nuance that you are likely to encounter, but at an assessment centre how much would you actually remember? Instead, I have covered everything you will need and are likely able to remember, including top tips for each stage. The first tip is to make use of the materials available from the College of Policing website along with those at the back of the book to practice with. The Army has a term 'train hard fight easy,' the same applies here. Put the time in to prepare - it will make an already stressful process much easier, along with boosting your confidence levels. Another Army term I like is, 'keep it simple, stupid,' whilst not completely diverse, what it says is to try and not over complicate things. Keep your examples on your application form and at the assessment centre simple. Use simple ideas on your written exercises at the assessment centre. Rather than saying, "I will hire a hundred more security guards." Could you not simply make better use of the ones you already have at the shopping centre. Position at key points or put extra patrols on at times where a pattern of more crime or criminal damage has been observed? After all, the Police does not have an unlimited budget and nor will the scenario at the assessment centre. As this would quite simply be unrealistic.
Rather than use police jargon, I have tried to write a guide that anyone can pick up, read and understand the process. Police jargon and being too 'policy' have actually caused many a candidate to fail. Stay clear of any jargon.
I still remember the candidate in their late teens coming out, red faced from a role play. They had tried to argue in the role play, thinking they were a police officer and ended up with a grade 'D' for working with others – an automatic fail for the whole assessment regardless of the grades he scored elsewhere. This

book has been structured to take you through the process step by step. With important aspects broken down into relevant sections and example questions included throughout the book as well as the back of the book to give you a chance to practice and gain valuable experience.

# How Will This Guide Help?

Many argue, that the current recruitment system is unfair and not diverse enough. The problem is, the current system is used to address two issues. The first is the volume of applicants applying to become a police officer. The second is to ensure applicants have the right aptitude and competencies to undertake the role. The best way to see if someone could do the job, would be to put them in a uniform and send them out on the street to see how they do. Obviously, this could cause a whole plethora of issues for those not able to cope or not the right type of person. The only other way to test to see if someone has the skills, is to test them by asking questions and getting them to undertake tasks in a sterile environment. This is where the application form CBQs start the process. They are there to see if someone has had experiences that show some of the competencies in a written format. In effect you write a short story, outlining key points connected with the question.

If successful at the CBQ stage, you will then find yourself at an assessment centre. Here you are tested further to see if you have the right aptitude and moral grounding to be a police officer or PCSO. It also puts a candidate under pressure to perform to a set standard. The 'fair' element is that everyone takes the same recruitment process and is marked to the same standards. However the examiners are all human and on numerous occasions I have heard people talking of differences in marking, in particular the CBQs.

The unfair element that some perceive; is that under pressure many potentially excellent candidates crack or cannot perform. Some have even been known to walk out half way through or even not turn up at all. Maybe, though, if they crack up at an

assessment centre, what would they do at a fatal RTC (Road Traffic Collision) or in the midst of numerous people fighting? This guide takes you through all the requirements you need to pass recruitment from the application to the final interview that some forces require. Offering an inside view into the whole recruitment process and the system the police use. All you need to do is read and then put into practice what you have learnt using the examples at the back of the book. The College of Policing website also has example material, which you can download and used to practice with, including the preparation material that is sent out to a candidate at least two weeks prior to their assessment centre. The example scenarios used in the role play and written assessment are particularly useful. You will notice the word preparation comes up quite a bit throughout the book! Once you understand what the assessors are looking for, you will find that when using the preparation material the answers will start to jump out at you and become quite obvious.
But more than anything, the better prepared and informed you are, your chance of success at each stage rises exponentially. I failed the application CBQs on my first attempt and passed both the application and assessment centre on my second attempt. All I did differently the second time around was to prepare and think about both the application form phase and the assessment centre, having the belief that the second time around I would pass if, I put extra effort in. I re-wrote the CBQ questions using the feedback from my first application to refine and improve. I rehearsed my structured interview answers, undertook several role plays and worked on my weak areas. All it took was time and effort. If you really want to be a police officer it will be all worth it when you pass the application form and then pass the assessment centre on your first attempt.

This book also covers special constable, PCSO as well as the police constable application process. The process is now very similar for all three, with standardized application forms, with only the score required to be higher for PCSO and then higher still for police constable. Also the special constable application form has two CBQs, PCSO three and police constable four. The assessment centre standards again is higher for Police Constable and PCSO than Special Constable. The Special Constable Assessment Centre is usually undertaken at the for you are applying to.

If you can understand what is being looked for and the mechanism used to asses, you can then prepare your responses by thinking through in advance. Ensuring your responses meet the requirements. The police use competency based questions not just in front line officer roles, but also for police staff. A competency based question is one where you are asked a question and your answer is based on an example from your past experience, which shows a certain skill or skills being looked for. In many ways they are quite straight forward as long as you have a good strong response that meets the required competency. This response is an example when you have displayed a skill or skills, such as diffusing conflict, challenging unacceptable behaviour, working to a tight deadline. As well as the example the idea is YOU state the circumstance, what you did (action), and the result with the bonus ball if you like, being to show a positive outcome. This is the first part many do not understand or overlook in the recruitment process.

Many of those that apply, especially for police constable, apply on a whim or with very little thought or preparation to the application process. They have maybe thought they would like to be a police officer, but not really given much thought to the actual job role and what they will undertake. They have very little

knowledge of the force they are applying to and undertake little research. So even after passing the application form and the assessment centre they then fail the final interview. With most forces this will mean starting the recruitment process over again after a sixth month wait.
Those that have not sufficiently prepared are the ones that are most likely to not make it through the recruitment process, which is tough, especially to those not prepared or know what to expect. Whilst the process is designed to select those with the necessary qualities, very few have the ability to show the qualities naturally in a more pressured environment.
Some do not think about the role of a police officer and what it entails. The role of a police officer has become more and more about customer service and being able to resolve situations. Both of these are key to the recruitment process and tested at the assessment centre. Again, I shall reiterate, understand the process and what is being looked for and you are half way there to achieving the grade required to pass. With a bit of prior preparation, you can gain a score much higher than required, aiding your chances of success. Especially, if the force you apply for, decide to take only the top 30 assessment centre scores for example by top slicing. An average recruitment can see around 2000 applicants for 60 to 100 posts. This makes the process extremely competitive and I cannot stress enough, that if you are serious, you need to prepare and put a large number of hours in completing your application, if successful at that stage then preparing for the assessment centre. Better still start preparing for the assessment centre, before you even apply. Good preparation and understanding the process could see an overall 10% improvement on your assessment centre grade, the difference between a pass or a fail. The skills you will learn are transferable to any job you are likely to apply for, as being polite and

courteous as well as understanding the role you are applying for, are key skills for many job applications and interviews.
Many of the skills required to be shown during the recruitment process; you either have experienced or have naturally. Some may need to work on their skills to ensure they shine through during the assessment centre. Whilst age is no barrier, the one small barrier for those of a younger age can mean that some don't always have good examples for the CBQs and structured interview questions at the assessment centre. Being able to understand and reflect on your strengths and weaknesses is a good starting point, then match these with the recruitment process to see what areas you need to improve to ensure you pass. Think of slightly difficult situations where you have had to problem solve, make a decision, diffuse conflict, persuade a work colleague or acquaintance to change their attitude or mind.
One very important element to realise, is being able to communicate succinctly and politely even under a stressful situation without becoming angry. Listening and not overtalking. Another is challenging discriminatory behaviour, rather than overlooking it. For some it may be that they don't understand the wide range of discriminatory behaviour. Your written English may be poor, or the ability to problem solve. Everything can be improved with a little time and effort. You will get out and achieve the results almost directly from the amount of effort you put into the preparation for the assessment centre and completion of the application form.
Hopefully, by reading this book you will have a better understanding of the recruitment process and what is being looked for at each stage of the process. This book not only covers the recruitment process but also gives you some key background, on the role of a police officer, to help you understand and generate answers to questions you may be asked. The many TV

cop shows splashed across our screens often miss out the many hours of paperwork a police officer will undertake. A witness statement can take a couple of hours, an arrest may take around four hours to complete all the necessary paperwork required by the CPS. The correct handling of a situation often has a big bearing on the outcome. Staying calm and not getting angry, even when being shouted at or threatened is another expectation of a police officer, PCSO or special constable. This will more often than not lead to a positive outcome, which is what is constantly being assessed during the recruitment process – what did you do to ensure a positive outcome.

Like many things in life, there is no magic formula, but you can give yourself the best chance possible with good preparation and prior knowledge. The final element is putting what you have learnt into practice…

## So You Want to join the police?

A Police officer is a warranted employee of a police force. Police officers are generally responsible for apprehending criminals, maintaining public order, and preventing and detecting crimes. Police officers are sworn to an oath, and are granted the power to arrest and imprison suspects, along with other practices.
You can either decide to join as a full-time police officer or become a volunteer officer known as a Special Constable. Both hold the office of constable and have the same warranted powers in England and Wales.
PCSOs are civilian members of police staff. They work alongside their police officer colleagues to provide a highly visible, accessible and familiar presence on the streets of villages, towns and cities. PCSOs engage with local communities, building bridges with the public. They are trained problem solvers, a reassuring presence and a deterrent against crime. They also support front line policing in non-confrontational roles, maintain order in public places, address low-level anti-social behaviour and tackle youth-disorder. They gather intelligence and work to reassure the public and make communities safer. PCSOs are not warranted, although are given various powers to undertake their role. They have no powers of arrest, but if given the power can detain and undertake various aspects of a police officer's role. It is becoming more and more a stepping stone into a police constable role for many wanting to join the police.

### *Short Self-Aptitude Test*

Here is a very short test to see if you have the aptitude to be a police officer or PCSO. Go down the list and choose the course of action you would take.
Question 1

You are on patrol alone at 1.30 am and passing the 'Bright Light' nightclub. You see a group of 10 young men outside the club. Suddenly there is a shout and a man is thrown to the ground. The group of 10 young men start to kick him violently in the head. You can see he is, almost immediately, rendered unconscious and is receiving blows to his head that will cause serious injury, or worse.

A Report what is happening by radio and request back up
B Observe and gather evidence of what happens
C Approach the crowd and shout: 'Police, police – get back!'
D Call for an ambulance because he is likely to be injured
E Draw your baton and body strike the attackers with as much force as is possible

Question 2

You are on patrol alone on a Saturday afternoon at 2 pm and the publican of the Grapes public house flags you down. He tells you there is a fight in his pub. You look through the door and notice there are about 60 people fighting each other. Furniture is being thrown across the bar and substantial damage has been caused.

A Call for backup and observe what is happening
B Go into the pub, shout at them and ask them to stop fighting
C Tell the licensee to close the pub immediately
D Book the licensee for keeping a disorderly house
E Go in and arrest the first person you see fighting

Question 3

You are on patrol with your Sergeant at 8.30 pm. You are passing a young Chinese man walking along the pavement and the sergeant instructs you to stop and search him. You ask the sergeant on what grounds. He replies, "Because he's Chinese"

A Refuse to do it and confront the Sergeant about his racist comments

B Stop and search the man on suspicion of having stolen property
C Refuse to do it because being 'Chinese' is not a ground to justify the stop and search.
D Stop and search the man and later report the Sergeant for being racist
E Tell the Chinese man, why the sergeant wanted him stopped and encourage him to make a formal complaint
Question 4
You attend a burglary in a confectionery shop at 3.00 am one morning with another constable. While you await the arrival of the owner your colleague picks up a bag of sweets, opens it and begins to eat them.
A Ask him if he is going to pay for the sweets when the owner arrives
B Ask your colleague for a sweet
C Pretend you didn't see what happened
D Arrest your colleague for stealing the sweets
E Do nothing and report the incident to your sergeant when you get back to the station
Question 5
You attend a domestic dispute at 2.00 am on your own. As you arrive you notice all the lights are on in the house, the front window has been smashed and music is blaring out. You look through the window and see a man. He spots you and immediately grabs a woman by the hair and puts a carving knife to her throat and says, "Get back copper or I'll slice her throat."
A Back off slightly, start talking to him and try to defuse the situation
B Rush into the house and strike the man with your baton to save the woman

C Do what he says and back off from the window so he cannot see you
D Immediately call for backup on your radio
E Call for an ambulance and armed response vehicle
Question 6
You are sitting in the canteen when you overhear two sergeants making sexist and derogatory comments about a woman officer and joking about her being a lesbian.
A Challenge the behaviour and ask them to stop
B Report them to a senior officer
C Ignore the comments
D Smile and laugh at the comments you hear
E Tell someone about it later
Question 7
Whilst on foot patrol at 1.30 pm in the High Street you receive a radio message to indicate that a member of the public has seen a man brandishing a handgun. The description of the man given fits perfectly a man walking about 25 feet in front of you.
A Confirm the description and follow him at a discrete distance
B Approach the man and demand he hands over the gun
C Jump him from behind and disarm him
D Do nothing, it is too risky
E Follow him and observe what he does
Question 8
You are on foot patrol with another colleague who stops to speak to a beggar. Suddenly, the beggar jumps up and punches her in the face. She falls to the ground and the beggar kicks her.
A Restrain and arrest the beggar using reasonable force
B Draw your baton and beat the beggar into submission
C Ask the beggar to stop
D Call for assistance
E Call an ambulance

Question 9
You are off duty and attend a party at a friend's house. There are 15 people at the party who are not police officers. When you get into the house you notice a number of people are smoking cannabis, some are popping ecstasy tabs and a couple are 'chasing the dragon' in the kitchen.
A Telephone the duty sergeant at the local police station, report the situation
B Ignore the drug taking and enjoy yourself
C Confront the people, tell them who you are and ask them to stop
D Try the drugs yourself
E Do nothing and report the incident later
Question 10
You attend a nightclub with a police colleague when you are off duty. As you approach the doorman your colleague takes out his warrant card and flashes it. The doorman turns to the cashier and says' "It's OK, they can go in free they are police."
A Challenge your colleague's behaviour and refuse to enter the club
B Enter the night club without paying
C Challenge your colleagues behaviour, then enter the club for free
D Buy the doorman a drink for being so generous
E Insist that you both pay the going rate
If you answered mainly A for all the questions you have strong potential to be a police officer!

## *Police Constable*

Full-time or regular officers undertake pretty much the same roles and duties as special constables, although being full time they often deal with much more serious crime. The obvious other big difference is special constables are volunteers and unpaid. I have often said that special constables tend to do all the visible side of a police officer – responding to incidents, making arrests, visible patrols etc. The other half of the job - building files, various reports, interviews, answering bail and statements are normally undertaken by full-time officers. Some investigations for what is called volume crime can still take days or even weeks, something a special constable unless one of the few working full-time hours would not be able to undertake.

Possibly, only being on duty once a week, a special constable will often do all the basic enquiries, but have to hand it on, to enable further investigation. Regular officers can also undertake training that is not available to special constables and can move into specialist roles not available to special constables. The options open to them during their career are wider and much more varied. All police officers start as police constables regardless of age and experience. Then after they have a two year probationary period before they can apply to join maybe Traffic, Armed response, Police Dogs Unit, or a Beat Manager for those that want to stay in uniform. The exception is some of the accelerated programs. Some police officers may be trained in special duties such as; counterterrorism, surveillance, child protection, VIP protection, and investigation techniques into major crime, such as fraud, rape, murder or drug trafficking.

### *Police Constables Pay as of 1st September 2015*

0 - £19,514 (a)
1 - £22,660 (b)
2 - £23,695 (c)
3 - £24,725
4 - £25,755
5 - £27,816

6 - £31,971
7 - £37,622
(a) Pay point 0 is the entry point for a member appointed in the rank of constable, unless the chief officer of police, after consultation with the local policing body, assigns the member to pay point 1 on the basis of policing qualifications, relevant experience or local recruitment needs. The salary paid to a member at pay point 0 shall be between £19,380 and £22,439 as determined by the chief officer of police, after consultation with the local policing body, on the basis of policing qualifications, relevant experience or local recruitment needs. Some forces automatically pay student officers at pay point 1, others expect at least 1 or 2 years' service as a PCSO, police staff, special constable or volunteer some a Substantive Special Constable or PCSO with 12-18 months service. Other pre-requisites imposed by some forces is the Certificate in Knowledge of Policing. It is best to check with the force you are applying to the HR department if you could qualify or a higher starting salary.
(b) On completion of basic training, a member who entered at pay point 0 will move to pay point 1.
(c) All members will move to pay point 2 after one full year at pay point 1, and progression will continue to be at a rate of one pay point per full year of service thereafter.
Alongside the main pay scale under the Windsor review was the addition of an unsocial hour bonus that will be paid pro rata for the hours worked between 8pm and 6am. For a constable this is up to £1400 for a constable working a standard eight-hour alternating shift pattern.

### *Certificate in Knowledge of Policing*

The Certificate in Knowledge of Policing is a modular qualification, made up of 10 units at Level 3 on the Qualifications and Credit Framework. It involves approximately 300 hours of study, of which about 100 hours are directed learning and the rest is made up of home study.

It is assessed through a mixture of methods, including tests, open-book assignments and closed-book assignments. A range of delivery options are available, including full-time, part-time, evenings only, weekends only and distance learning. Various colleges and private training firms deliver the course.

The Certificate in Knowledge of Policing gives you an understanding of policing and police law, and enables you to demonstrate some of the critical decision-making skills required for the job. It covers a wide range of subjects, including:

Using police powers in a fair and just way

Social and community issues and neighbourhood policing

Responding to incidents and providing initial support to victims and witnesses

Searching premises and searching individuals within a policing context

Participating in planned policing operations

Interviewing witnesses and suspects

Victim support

The criminal justice system

Legislation, policy and guidelines.

Achieving the qualification will help prepare you for recruitment to the police service as a police constable in England or Wales. Successful achievement of the qualification does not guarantee recruitment as a student police constable. However, it does show a dedication to joining the police, and is relevant to other roles in the criminal justice sector.

Every police force in England and Wales sets its own recruitment process and selection policy, and entry requirements vary from force to force. The Metropolitan Police is the first police force to require new police officer candidates to achieve the qualification before they apply. Other forces are following suit. The Met however, does not expect substantive special constables to undertake the qualification. The cost of the qualification is between £500 and £1000, and funding for the course may be available as a loan or bursary.

### *Shift Pattern*

Being a police officer is a 24 hour 7 days a week, 365 days a year job. That is broken down into shift work and an example of a typical set of shifts might be:
2 days 7 until 4pm
2 days 3 until 12am
2 days 10pm until 7am
Followed by 4 days off.
As can be seen, you work at all hours of the day and night at weekends, even Christmas day. The shifts can be difficult to get used to, and your first night shift can feel like the longest night ever. They may even be an impact on your life in terms of things you use to do regularly might not always fit into your shift pattern. Partners may need to adjust to not seeing you as they may well be at work whilst you are sleeping. All this can take its toll on your social and personal life. On other occasions may have to stay on duty due to an incident or having to complete essential paperwork. This can impinge on pre-planned events. PCSOs also have their own shift pattern most only work till 10pm or midnight, as opposed to through the night. They can get paid overtime or have time off in lieu just like a police constable if required to stay on or opt to do extra hours for an operation.
As a Special Constable you will more often than not choose when you want to go on duty, to fit around work commitments or other officers shift patterns. One tip is that if working with full-

time officers, always try to work a full shift with them. There may be times when you were due to get off, but end up staying on due to a serious incident or simply needing to complete paperwork. It really is not a job that you can just finish at a set time, and walk away from at a set time on occasions. Imagine being at an RTC controlling the traffic and deciding to just go off duty. What would happen to the traffic? Always worth considering, if maybe you need to be up early for work the next day or have pre-planned event to attend.

Beat Managers or constables working within the NPT teams may work slightly different hours some working till just 12-1am and doing two weekends out of every four.

A local police force will deal with emergencies and non-emergencies within certain agreed times and if you've been a victim of crime, they will agree with you how often and for how long you will be kept informed of progress on your case.

All Police forces across the whole of the England and Wales have signed up to provide the same level of service to their communities. This means that it will be easier for the public to have their say on how they police, the local area, and guarantees that wherever they live, they can expect the same, high level of service.

Wherever anybody lives, they can get the following information by searching for their neighbourhood policing team on their force website:

Contact details of the Neighbourhood Policing Team

Details of the next Neighbourhood Policing meeting

The neighbourhood priorities

Action being taken by the police and follow-up to problems raised by the community

Local crime statistics, information and crime maps

How to get involved and help make your community safer

### *Special Constable*

To be eligible, you must meet the following basic criteria:
You must be a national of a country within the European Economic Area or, if a national of a country outside the EEA, have the right to reside in this country without restrictions.
You must be 18 years of age or over.
You cannot be working in an occupation that would conflict with your duties as a Special Constable. Some of these occupations include: Traffic Warden, Security, Licensee, private detective, and magistrate. Anything that may bring you into conflict with your role as a Police officer is worth checking. Contact your local force for their list if you feel your current job may be an issue.
If you meet the criteria you can either contact the local force directly, or speak to the Specials recruitment officer. Many constabularies have downloadable application forms and information on their website. You can simply fill out the form, print and post or email it to the recruitment section of the force you are applying to.
As a special, most forces will expect you to be willing to undertake duty time to the equivalent of a minimum of four hours per week, which is the standard minimum. You must be willing to undertake an initial training course and attend regular training at your chosen division or station, in order to maintain your skills.
As a serving Special Constable you will personally benefit from:
New experiences – you can expect to enjoy much of the variety that comes along with police work.
New people – you will be working as one of a team and the experiences you share in working closely together can lead to lasting friendships. You will learn more about life and human nature than most people will ever see.

New skills – you will learn new skills and develop existing ones, such as problem solving, negotiating, decision-making, coping with pressure, communications and inter-personal skills. These skills will help you not only as a Special, but also in your daily life, as well as in your current workplace. This will be supported by the forces' appraisal system.

Most forces will pay your travelling expenses from home or work, to your Police station, and offer a boot allowance of £50-70 or more. Some forces were running bounty schemes for the completion of set hours or objectives. An example is a £500 tax deductible bounty for doing 300 or more duty hours in a year. A few of these schemes have been disbanded as the police cuts have meant money has had to be re-directed into to training and such like.

Being a special can be one of the most exciting ways to volunteer, and find out about the role of a police officer. Being a Special Constable does not guarantee you will get in as a full-time officer, but it will help with scenarios and an awareness of the role of a Police Officer. You will also find existing officers will be very happy to help you complete your full-time application and give you tips. Some forces run awareness sessions for the application process, to aid your application and give important tips and pitfalls in the application process.

### *Special Constabulary Role*

The Special Constabulary mainly forms part of the neighbourhood policing teams, working alongside regular police officers, PCSOs and their partners. Although they are now more and more working with reactive or response units, CID, traffic and PSU. The primary role of the Special Constabulary is specifically to provide a high visibility presence (therefore

reducing the fear of crime), dealing with anti-social behaviour and gathering and acting upon community intelligence.
A Special Constable is normally part of the neighbourhood team, as part of a larger government initiative. Some Specials do all of their time with these teams whilst some do a proportion of their time with them and the rest being spent with what is known as Response or Reactive. These are the police officers who respond to 999 calls from the public which can be anything from a Road Traffic Collision (RTC) to a fight at a local pub or a theft from a shop.
Any constabulary will ensure that you are fully trained to deal with policing problems that are affecting local communities. As a Special Constable you hold the same powers as a full-time officer – powers throughout the whole of England and Wales.

### *PCSO*

A police community support officer (PCSO) or community support officer (CSO) is a civilian member of police staff employed as a uniformed non-warranted officer by one of the forty-three territorial police forces in England and Wales or the British Transport Police, which is the only special police force to employ PCSOs. PCSOs were introduced in September 2002 and first recruited by the Metropolitan Police under the Police Reform Act 2002 that was given Royal Assent by Queen Elizabeth II on 24 July 2002. There are currently 15,820 PCSOs in England and Wales. PCSO numbers have, like those of police constables, been falling in recent years due to economic austerity, although recruitment has started again to replace those that have left or progressed onto a police constable role. At their peak in 2009, 16,814 PCSOs were employed. PCSOs represent 6.8% of total police employees in England and Wales. The Metropolitan Police has the highest contingent of PCSOs, accounting for a quarter of PCSOs nationally. Pay for PCSOs varies from force to force from between around £16,000 to around £27,000 per year, taking into account a shift allowance or working unsocial hours (from 8pm until 6am and weekends). Most PCSOs work within a Safer Neighbourhood Team (SNT) or Neighbourhood Policing Team (NPT) that contains PCSOs, special constables and beat managers. Day-to-day duties usually include high visibility patrolling, tackling anti-social behaviour, dealing with minor offences, gathering criminal intelligence and supporting front-line policing. The Home Office has specifically limited the powers designated to PCSOs to maintain the distinction between them and police officers. Some PCSOs are attached to Road Policing Units, and British Transport Police PCSOs are deployed as part of station teams. As with many aspects of PCSOs, the specifics of each job description vary depending on the relevant force and the powers granted by the chief constable.

### *Neighbourhood Policing*

Neighbourhood Policing is a style of policing that provides communities with a visible, familiar, and accessible policing team who work in partnership with other agencies, such as Council Street Wardens, licensing, local/parish council to reduce crime and anti-social behaviour and address local community safety priorities. All forces are committed to neighbourhood policing within their respective areas.

As such, teams are made up of regular police officers, PCSOs who work on the front-line alongside Special Constables, and Beat Managers. PCSO's provide a visible and reassuring presence on the streets and tackling the menace of anti-social behaviour. PCSOs have different roles in different forces, but they usually patrol a beat and interact with the public, while also offering assistance to police officers at crime scenes and major events.

Depending on where they work, they could: deal with minor offences offer early intervention to deter people from committing offences provide support for front-line policing conduct house-to-house enquiries guard crime scenes provide crime prevention advice.

Although, PCSOs do not have the same powers as regular police officers, they still carry a lot of responsibility, and are a crucial part of the police force. Along with Special Constables, they have been established to work with their partners to ensure the right people, the right numbers and with the right skills, are in the right place at the right time. The size of each team depends on the local community needs. Members of the team concentrate on resolving local problems, such as disruptive families, drug misuse and anti-social behaviour.

One of the keys to effective neighbourhood policing is active engagement, consultation and communication with local people to ensure their interests and concerns are reflected in the delivery of policing, community safety and neighbourhood services. Local meetings or "Beat Surgeries" are organised so locals can have a voice.

Due to the unpredictable nature of law enforcement, police officers can encounter many dangerous situations in the course of their career. Officers face an increased risk of infectious diseases, physical injury, or in some cases, death, as well as the potential for emotional disorder due to both the high stress and inherently adversarial nature of police work. These dangers are encountered in many different situations, such as the investigation, pursuit, and apprehension of criminals, motor vehicle stops, crimes, response to terrorism, and intervention in domestic disputes, investigating traffic accidents, and directing traffic. The constant risk, uncertainty and tension inherent in law enforcement and the exposure to vast amounts of human suffering and violence can lead susceptible individuals to anxiety, depression, and alcoholism.

Individuals are drawn to police work for many reasons. Among these often include a desire to protect the public and social order from criminals and danger. A desire to hold a position of respect and authority; a disdain for or antipathy towards criminals and rule breakers; the professional challenges of the work; the employment benefits that are provided with civil service jobs in many countries; the sense of camaraderie that often holds among police; or a family tradition of police work or civil service. An important task of the recruitment activity of police agencies is screening potential candidates to determine the fitness of their character and personality for the work. Often through background investigations and consultation with a psychologist. Even though Police work is very dangerous, police officers are still seen by most people as necessity to maintain order. However, there are also those that dislike the police Force and what it stands for. Becoming a police officer may mean losing friends as well as gaining new ones.

## Recruitment Process

The recruitment process can take several months, even more than a year for police constables. It may be at least 6 months or up to eighteen between applying and actually starting training. It is important to be patient and use the time in between each process to study and prepare or the next stage. This also includes fitness training, in preparation for the fitness test usually undertaken towards the end of the process. The process is very similar for both full-time officers, PCSOs and special constables - the special constable process can vary slightly from force to force. Specials do not usually have such a rigorous application form or assessment day. Their assessment is usually undertaken at a weekend or weekday evening locally. However, the process always includes elements from the police constable recruitment assessment day, such as structured interview, Physcsemetric/PIRT and written exercises. Your force will send you a recruitment pack outlining what their recruitment consists of and then you can refer to those specific elements in this chapter. One important point is that you are only allowed to apply for one force at a time and there is a minimum time limit of 6 months allowed between each application if you are not successful.

### *National Specials Recruit Assessment Process*

The National Specials Recruit Assessment Process is a rigorous one involving the observation of candidates' performance across a variety of exercises, assessing their potential to perform the role effectively.

Key features of the assessment process are:

Assessments are made on what candidates do and how they do it

Trained assessors evaluate each candidate's performance in exercises which relate to identified core competencies

Information from all of the exercises is used to produce the final results.
Assessment exercises include:
A written exercise lasting 20 minutes
A situational judgment test lasting 65 minutes
A competency-based structured interview with 4 questions lasting 20 minutes in total.
As I said, Specials recruitment is not quite as standardised as regular officer recruitment and can vary between forces. With this in mind, the NPIA (National Police Improvement Agency), now the College of Policing, developed a National Recruitment Process and Standards for the Special Constabulary. The new process and standards were formally approved for national rollout from 1 April 2010 by the Special Constabulary National Consultative Group (SCNCG). With the recruitment of Special Constables has been a local matter, which meant that each of the 43 forces could be running different recruitment processes and using different standards. However, since the launch of the National Strategy for the Special Constabulary in March 2008, the NPIA was working with its partners to produce national standards and an assessment process, with the College of Policing taking this on and introducing a standardised application form, from May 2013, which is the same as the PCSO and the police constable application form. The differences are having two instead of four CBQs on the Special Constable, three on the PCSO and four CBQs on the Police Constable Application form. All forces are now using this new application form and current six skills and assessment centre format.
Rollout of the new special recruitment began on 1st April 2010. The NPIA provided each force that adopted the new process with two training courses (assessor training and Quality Assurance training) and other support free of charge during the

rollout period. The College of Policing then took over from the NPIA and have further tweaked and supported a more standardised recruitment of specials, including the IL4SC (Intial Learning 4 Special Constables) to standardise special constable training, as the case with the IPLDP (Initial Police Learning and Development Program) for police constables.
The assessment exercises are based on the competencies from the Skills for Justice Framework. This Framework is a series of national standards which sets out, amongst other things, the competencies required for each role within the police force, including that of Special Constable. These competencies are covered later in the chapter.
Forces should also apply the same fitness, medical and eyesight standards as apply to regular officers. Candidates are required to take the following two fitness tests:
Dynamic Strength test (upper-body strength). This requires the candidate to perform seated chest pushes and five seated back pulls on a specially designed device
Endurance fitness. This endurance fitness test involves running to and fro on a 15 metre track in time with a series of bleep

### *Police Constable Application*

A typical application process for full-time officers is laid out below. Anything after the application phase can vary between different forces. Although some forces use an online filtering system before issuing an application form, others have the force interview prior to going to the assessment centre. It is always worth reading what the process is.
Initial Application including four CBQs which are assessed.
Assessment day.
Security vetting of yourself, your immediate family, and any other adults who may live at your address.

Fitness Test.
An interview.
A full medical.
Of those that apply, only 15% are successful at becoming a Police officer and many have had to apply several times to get in. If you do not succeed on your first attempt, ensure you get feedback and the re-apply. Don't get disheartened and don't give up. Reading this book alone will ensure you are better prepared than the majority of those who apply. Many apply on a whim or with little thought or preparation to the application process. The CBQs on the application form alone take many hours of drafting ad tweaking, the assessment centre does require you to pre-read fully the supplied scenario information. Understanding how the assessment day is undertaken and what to expect is another. The better prepared you are for each stage the more likely you are to pass each stage.
The application form in itself is very important, 60%-70% of applicants for the role of police officer and PCSO are rejected at the application form stage. You are marked and graded on your answers to the competency questions and getting these right is a key element of your application form. Most forces want a score of 9 or 10 but some require a score of 11 for PC or 8 or 9 for PCSO. It is a competitive process due to the way the grades are scored using the highest and lowest score achieved from a batch of candidates, then the A, B, C, D grade is applied. An overall grade B or a B for each of the CBQs. The questions ask you to give examples that meet with the seven core competencies and we will cover these later. In addition, your eligibility requirements will be checked before your application can go to the next stage.
You can even fail on using blue instead of black ink, not following the guidelines properly and even incorrect spelling, grammar and punctuation. As all these things, relate back to the

six core competencies that you will cover later. Expect to spend around twelve hours or more completing the application form, including writing your competency answers. Getting this stage wrong could mean being rejected and having to wait 6 months before you can apply. The time you put in will pay dividends. If unsuccessful, make sure you get feedback so that you know what to improve next time. Again, don't be disheartened, some of the best police officers I have worked with applied four times before they passed recruitment. Some have failed the paper sift others have had to go through the SEARCH assessment centre two or even three times. Each time, though you gain valuable experience and with feedback you will be able to correct any failings and understand how to play the 'game' in terms of showing the correct skills at the right time during the recruitment process.

***Eligibility Requirements***

Eligibility requirements for the police are fairly detailed listed is the main criterion that needs to be met. The criteria is the same for all the operational roles of special constable, PCSO and a police constable.

Age requirements Applications can be accepted at the age of 18. There's no upper age limit for applying to the Police service, but bear in mind that the normal retirement age is 60 years and that new recruits are required to undertake a two-year probationary period.

Nationality requirements, you must be a British citizen, an EC/EEA national or a Commonwealth citizen or foreign national with no restrictions on your stay in the United Kingdom. Foreign nationals and UK citizens who have lived abroad may have to wait some time for security and vetting clearance. All applicants have to be vetted to the same standard before appointment.

Criminal record - A number of crimes will mean a definite or likely rejection of your application, including anyone who has received a formal caution in the last five years, committed a violent crime or public order offence.
Tattoos, which could cause offence. Tattoos are not acceptable if they are particularly prominent, garish, and offensive or undermine the dignity and authority of your role. You will be asked to disclose any tattoos on a separate form.
Applicants will have their financial status checked. These checks are carried out because police officers have access to privileged information, which may make them vulnerable to corruption. Applicants with outstanding County court judgments, who have been registered bankrupt with outstanding debts, will be rejected. If you have discharged bankruptcy debts then you will need to provide a Certificate of Satisfaction with your application.
Police constable applicants must have a Level 3 qualification, like an A Level, BTEC national or equivalent to be eligible to apply. If unsure, check with the force you intend to apply to that it meets the requirements. The Certificate in Policing Knowledge does meet the requirements for a level 3 qualification.
To ensure you are fit enough for the role, you will undertake a fitness test. There are two elements to the test and you must pass both before you can be appointed. They are looking for no more than the minimum standard needed, to enable you to work effectively as a police officer. You will be given help to improve your fitness and if you prepare yourself properly, there is no reason for you to fail.
There are two elements to the test: dynamic strength and endurance fitness, and health.
Police officers and PCSOs encounter stressful situations, trauma, physical confrontation and work long hours on shifts. They need to be resilient enough to cope with the demands and pressures of

Police work. Applicants must therefore be in good health mentally and physically to undertake Police duties.
You will undergo a medical examination to ensure you meet the health standards required.
Applicants will have their eyesight tested at the medical assessment stage. You may be asked to go to an optician to have your eyes tested and the eyesight form filled in. Failure to pass this test will lead to rejection.
You can only apply to one force at any one time. If you have previously applied to join the Police service and been unsuccessful, you must wait six months from your initial rejection before you can apply again. You can withdraw a current application to apply to another force, if you have passed the CBQs or assessment centre, then these grades can be transferred if the recruiting force is happy to accept them.
Applicants from all backgrounds and ethnic groups are encouraged to apply. Some forces offer positive action to help those from unrepresented groups. There may hold seminars to discuss the benefits of becoming a police officer. Some forces assign mentors to help but not complete the application process for underrepresented groups. Applicants are not limited to any particular age group, in fact; those who are looking for a career change are encouraged to join with valuable life experience. The minimum age to apply is 18, and there is no upper age limit, though you should bear in mind that the normal retirement age for Police Constables and sergeants is 60 at this present time, but in line with many other sectors will most likely rise. You should also be aware that all new recruits, whatever their age, are required to undertake a two-year probationary period before you can look towards any career advancement.

### *Get Fit Before You Apply*

One of the most rigorous elements of our screening process is the physical fitness training. Police Officers must be able to move quickly while carrying a lot of heavy equipment; they have to be in pretty good shape.

If you pass the assessment process, you will then have to take a physical fitness test. To pass, you will need to be reasonably fit, and able to run short distances fairly quickly. The bleep test is the most common test along with a grip test for the fitness element. Tis requires you to pass level 5.4 which is not that high, but may be a shock if you are not particularly fit. Later you will also have to pass a medical examination. All officers are now required to undertake an annual fitness test as part of their operational requirements. The test is also the same as the one that new recruits undertake as part of the recruitment process. Special Constables also now undertake an annual fitness test, the same as full-time officers.

### *Core Competencies/Skills*

These are the competencies/skills being looked at within your application, at the assessment centre and may come up in your interview. Whilst you do not need to score quite so highly on the special constable or PCSO application form or answer as many questions, the same process in terms of answering the question applies. Although, individual forces can opt for a higher score depending on the number and quality of the applications, as the only way to sift and reduce numbers going to the assessment centre.

You need to try and give examples of when and where you have dealt with each of them. You are graded on your responses. Try to think of good examples that illustrate each competence. Try not to waffle and just show exactly where you have come across

each competency in your day to day life. They don't have to be that current either. The aim is to look at your life experience and how you have reacted to each of the competencies. If you have experience of being a Special Constable or a PCSO these will often help you give good examples that you have experienced on duty. Many regular officers will be more than happy to offer advice and guidance by already be part of the police family. Another worthwhile point that is essential to the police force is political correctness and making sure you use the correct terminology and words that are not in any way sexist, racist or homophobic. Diversity is the key here.
Even though the application form says, "Typeface" some forces will disregard an application form submitted in typeface. However, there is now a MS Word version of the application form to be completed in typeface/electronically, which is to aid more electronic based applications, where the application form is emailed in, instead of posting it in. Handwriting, spelling, grammar and punctuation are tested at the assessment centre in two hand written exercises. The expectation is that more applications will be accepted electronically, even possibly filled out online. It is worth checking with the force you are applying to, if it is not made clear if application forms have to be handwritten or not.

### *Definition of Diversity*

The concept of diversity encompasses acceptance and respect. It means understanding that each individual is unique, and recognizing our individual differences. These can be along the dimensions of race, ethnicity, gender, sexual orientation, socio-economic status, age, physical abilities, religious beliefs, political beliefs, or other ideologies. It is the exploration of these differences in a safe, positive, and nurturing environment.

It is about understanding each other and moving beyond simple tolerance to embracing and celebrating the rich dimensions of diversity contained within each individual.

# CURRENT SIX SKILLS

Since, Nov 1, 2012, the seven competencies have been replaced by six skills based around the Skills for Justice police constable competencies, which are:

Decision making

Leadership

Service Delivery

Public service

Working with others

Public Service

Demonstrates a real belief in public service, focusing on what matters to the public and will best serve their interests. Understands the expectations, changing needs and concerns of different communities, and strives to address them. Builds public confidence by talking with people in local communities to explore their viewpoints and break down barriers between them and the police. Understands the impact and benefits of policing for different communities, and identifies the best way to deliver services to them. Works in partnership with other agencies to deliver the best possible overall service to the public.

One of the fundamental roles of the police is to serve the public and respond to their needs. You will be required to build confidence in the public as communities are now far more diverse than ever. You will need to gather intelligence and work with different agencies such as the Local Authority, the Fire Service and other stakeholders to provide a great public service. During the selection process, you must provide a really good service during the role plays and the written report writing. You may also get asked an interview question that goes along the lines of:

"Can you give an example of when you have delivered excellent customer service to a member of the public?"

Openness to change

Positive about change, adapting rapidly to different ways of working and putting effort into making them work. Flexible and open to alternative approaches to solving problems. Finds better, more cost-effective ways to do things, making suggestions for change. Takes an innovative and creative approach to solving problems.

The police force has been changing for many years now and they want to recruit new officers who are open to change. You will have to find better and more cost-effective ways of working in the police force and be open to the changes that are implemented by senior officers. During the selection process, you will have to answer questions based around your understanding of change and how it affects the force. This might be done during a police officer final interview if your chosen force decides to have one as part of the police selection process.

Service delivery

Understands the organisation's objectives and priorities, and how own work fits into these. Plans and organises tasks effectively, taking a structured and methodical approach to achieving outcomes. Manages multiple tasks effectively by thinking things through in advance, prioritising and managing time well. Focuses on the outcomes to be achieved, working quickly and accurately and seeking guidance when appropriate.

Effective service delivery is crucial to the police force. You will have to plan and organise your tasks to fit in with the police force's main objectives and goals. During the assessment centre you will have to organise your actions in the role play and interactive scenarios in order to demonstrate that you have this key quality. An interview question for the assessment centre might be:

"Can you give an example of when you have planned or organised an event to meet someone else's requirements?"

Professionalism

Acts with integrity, in line with the values and ethical standards of the Police Service. Takes ownership for resolving problems, demonstrating courage and resilience in dealing with difficult and potentially volatile situations. Acts on own initiative to address issues, showing a strong work ethic and demonstrating extra effort when required. Upholds professional standards, acting honestly and ethically, and challenges unprofessional conduct or discriminatory behaviour. Asks for and acts on feedback, learning from experience and developing own professional skills and knowledge. Remains calm and professional under pressure, defusing conflict and being prepared to step forward and take control when required.

Without doubt, this is one of the most important core competencies. The public expects its police officers to be professional at all times and uphold the principles of great service delivery. You will need to act with integrity and take ownership for resolving problems. In particular, during the police assessment centre role play scenarios you will have to act in a resilient manner and take action to solve any problems. You can demonstrate this by saying to the role play actor: "I can assure you that I will take personal responsibility for making things happen and I will act now in order to resolve this issue."

Decision making

Gathers, verifies and assesses all appropriate and available information to gain an accurate understanding of situations. Considers a range of possible options before making clear, timely, justifiable decisions. Reviews decisions in the light of new information and changing circumstances. Balances risks, costs and benefits, thinking about the wider impact of decisions.

Exercises discretion and applies professional judgement, ensuring actions and decisions are proportionate and in the public interest. As a police officer you will have to gather information from a range of sources in order to allow you to make effective decisions. Before making a decision you will need to consider all of the facts of the case. During the report writing stage of the selection process, you will have to read a summary of events in relation to the Westshire Centre and then come up with a written report solving the problem. Most candidates fail at this stage due to poor spelling and grammar. Make sure you practice these in the build-up to the assessment centre.

Working with others

Works co-operatively with others to get things done, willingly giving help and support to colleagues. Is approachable, developing positive working relationships. Explains things well, focusing on the key points and talking to people using language they understand. Listens carefully and asks questions to clarify understanding, expressing own views positively and constructively. Persuades people by stressing the benefits of a particular approach, keeps them informed of progress and manages their expectations. Is courteous, polite and considerate, showing empathy and compassion. Deals with people as individuals and addresses their specific needs and concerns. Treats people with respect and dignity, dealing with them fairly and without prejudice regardless of their background or circumstances.

Finally, as a police officer you will have to work with others as part of a team in order to solve problems. You will also have to offer support to your work colleagues and be flexible in your approach to tasks. Furthermore, you should be willing to work with anyone regardless of their age, sex, sexual orientation, religious beliefs or otherwise. The police force needs to be diverse in nature, if it is to provide an excellent service to the public. At the assessment centre if you get a grade D in working with others, you fail the entire assessment centre. Below are all six competencies with suggestions and keywords that can be incorporated into the CBQs, structured interview, roleplays and written exercises.

Public Service

- Focused on the customer at all times to ensure I delivered an excellent service.
- I addressed the needs of the person I was dealing with.
- I listened to their viewpoint.
- By speaking with them I was able to build their confidence in my abilities.
- I took the time to identify the best way to meet their needs.
- I worked alongside other people to ensure the best service was delivered.

Openness to change

- I was positive about the pending change.
- I took steps to adapt to the new working-practices.
- I put in extra effort to make the changes work.
- I was flexible in my approach to work.
- I searched for alternative ways to deal with the situation.
- I took an innovative approach to working with the new guidelines and procedures.

Service delivery

- I consider the organisations main objectives and aims whilst carrying out my work.
- Used an action plan to help me achieve the task.
- I was organised in my approach to the working situation.
- I managed a number of different tasks at once and ensured that my time-management was effective.
- I focused at all times on the end result.

- I asked for clarification whenever I was unsure.

Professionalism

- I acted at all times in a professional and ethical manner.
- I took responsibility for solving the problem.
- I stood by my decision despite the objections from others.
- I remained calm at all times and in control of the situation.
- I immediately challenged the inappropriate behaviour.
- In order to improve my performance I sought feedback from my manager.
- I took steps to defuse the conflict.
- I took control of the situation in order to achieve a positive outcome.

Decision Making

- I gathered all of the information available before making my decision.
- I verified that the information was accurate before using it to make a decision.
- I considered all possible options first.
- I reviewed my decision once the new information had become available.
- I considered the wider implications before making my decision.
- I remained impartial at all times.
- I considered the confidentiality of the information I was receiving.

Working with others

- I worked with the other members of the team to get the task completed.
- At all times I considered the other members of the team and offered my support whenever possible.
- I took steps to develop a positive working relationship with the other members of the team.

• I fully briefed the other members of the team on what we need to achieve.
• I adapted my style of communication to fit the audience.
• I listened to the other persons views and took them into consideration.
• I took positive steps to persuade the team to follow my course of action.
• I kept the others updated of my progress at all times.
• I addressed their needs and concerns immediately.
• At all times I treated the other with respect and dignity.

### *Police Constable Application Form*

The application form is maybe the first chance a police force will have at seeing what you are all about. It is a very long and detailed application form. Great care needs to be taken when filling it out. Any mistakes or not gaining the required B grade on the competency questions will mean at least a six month wait before you can re-apply. The national pass is a score of 9. However, forces with high application numbers and a plethora of candidates achieving 9 or greater can raise the score to 10 or 11 to top slice the required number for the assessment centre.
Remember that all questions are important, the first part of the application form is all about you. The next part consists of a series of questions, which are graded, police constable requiring he highest grade to pass. If you are not used to answering competency based questions, it can seem quite daunting at first. Some may feel using one of the many checking services worthwhile for the police constable application. These will not write your answers, but will check to see if they are good enough to pass and give pointers and corrections so they are at the required level to pass. The only downside is if you have only a short amount of time to get your application in. It makes for a

tight timescale and if looking to apply, getting your competency questions correct will help no end.
Hopefully, by having the actual questions listed below, you can start thinking about and formulating some ideas before you apply or get an application form. I cannot stress enough how important your answers to the competency questions are, which are covered in detail later on in the chapter. Having pre-written answers that you have spent time preparing in advance, will ensure you have high quality answers ready to insert even if you have a short deadline, in which to complete the application and submit it. Plenty of time spent writing and tweaking is the key. Then getting someone to proof read your application as you are only allowed a maximum of ten mistakes. It is far better to have none at all, if possible. Consider word processing them first. If you are handwriting your application, then you do need to think about how much space you have. Each question has around 4 lines for each element as a rough guide. The application is A4 size and a typed font size would be Time New Roman 14 for the CBQs. You cannot write outside the margins or on a continuation sheet for the CBQs.
The Special Constables application form asks for two CBQs (Q1, Q2). The pass mark is lower than the three on the PCSO (Q1, Q2, Q3) all four on the police constable application forms, although there may be some local variance. For all, filling out the application and answering the questions, should be the same process. Using the word, "I" not "we" making use of keywords in the core competencies for example.
The key to success in this part of the form is to understand the purpose of the questions, and to spend some time finding the best example in your life experiences to illustrate the point required. Many applicants simply write down a very brief and superficial experience, with no depth not bringing in key words or

phrases. These lead to a low score and the application being rejected. 75% of applicants fail at the application stage due to poor examples and not answering the questions properly. It is essential that the answer is as thorough as possible. As a simple guide, look at each question and consider the following.

### *Q1 – Professionalism*

Please describe a specific occasion when you have intervened to take control of a situation.
Why was it necessary to intervene in the situation?
What did you do to take control of the situation?
What did you consider when intervening in the situation?
What was particularly good or effective about how you intervened to take control of the situation?
What difficulties did you experience and how did you overcome them?

### *Q2 - Working with others*

Please describe a specific occasion when you have encouraged a person to view an issue more positively.
Why was it necessary to encourage the person to view the issue more positively?
How did you encourage the person to view the issue more positively?
What did you consider when encouraging the person to view the issue more positively?
What was particularly good or effective about how you encouraged the person to view the issue more positively?
What difficulties did you experience and how did you overcome them?

### *Q3 - Decision Making*

Please describe a specific occasion you have considered a number of options before making a decision?
Why was it necessary to consider a number of options before making the decision?
What did you consider when identifying options?
What did you consider when making the decision?
What was particularly good or effective about how you identified the options and made the decision?
What difficulties did you experience and how did you overcome them?

### *Q4 - Service Delivery*

Please describe a specific occasion when you have had to manage your time effectively in order to complete a task.
Why did you have to manage your time effectively in order to complete the task?
How did you manage your time effectively in order to complete the task?
What did you consider to make sure you completed the task?
What was particularly good or effective about how you managed your time?
What difficulties did you experience and how did you overcome them?
Firstly, try to identify what skill areas are being looked for by reading the question thoroughly. Think of a **Strong** example for each competency, they need to be something that is above what you may do day to day. A challenge or challenging situation is a good example, where you have had to take control/intervene/problem solve/persuade. They do not have to be police examples if you are a PCSO or special constable. The assessors are just looking for a good example that shows various

elements in each competency. Here are examples of the way to write your questions, notice the word 'I' and use of the odd keyword from the competency being assessed. Note these are quite generic just to give you an idea of how to write part of an answer.

Professionalism

What was particularly good or effective about how you intervened to take control of the situation?

I felt I dealt with the situation effectively because I remained calm and professional throughout. I demonstrated courage because the situation was becoming aggressive, yet despite this, I opted without being asked to intervene.

Working with Others

What was particularly good or effective about how you encouraged the person to view the issue more positively?

By asking them if they wanted my assistance in a friendly and clear way, this was effective because it demonstrated that I was there to help and I was a team player. They could rely on me when faced with difficult issues, even when it related to their work performance and I did not judge them.

Decision Making

What did you consider when identifying options?

I considered the impact factors of setting up a youth group. I had to understand the financial situation and individuals' needs and what would help the community the most. Anti-social behaviour had become a problem. The young people I spoke to said they were bored as had nothing to do in the evening. I needed to balance risk, costs and benefits.

Once you have thought of an example, outline briefly what the issue or the circumstances of the event were and jot down a few notes. See what parts of one the four competencies it covers by seeing which keywords/skills match the actions you re describing.

State what actions you carried out to address the issue.
Maybe Say what effect this had on the group or others.
Describe the result.
Describe how there was a positive outcome, in that the issue was solved and all parties had a positive learning experience from it.

### *CBQ Top Tips*

Use the word 'I' not 'we' after all the answers need to show what **YOU** did.

See where Keywords from the core competencies can be added and blended into your response, this will greatly improve your score as shows the assessor that you have met part of the competency.

For professionalism. Think about a situation you have had to take control of and step in without being asked. Maybe show courage by stepping in to resolve it. Staying calm whilst someone else is being volatile or aggressive towards you.

Make sure you do not just write a load of key words, but actually tell a short story, as the key words are only good if they connect to what **YOU** did. Always start with a quick description of the situation/event so the assessor knows

Do not use an experience from when you were a child, and do not specifically name people. Remember diversity and stay gender neutral unless appropriate to the situation that they were being picked on or bullied due to sex, religion, disability, sexual orientation or transgender.

Your examples must be specific. Don't generalise - use a situation that shows a strong response not something minor. At the same time they don't have to be earth shattering examples either.

Add positive phrases like, "I resolved the conflict by staying calm and explaining the situation.", "I focused on the outcome by putting an action plan in place." "I took responsibility." "I stepped in without being asked to."

Explain why it would not be good to behave in a negative manner for a keyword, "I knew getting **angry** would not be the best way to resolve a **volatile situation**." Explain what would of happened had you not intervened, taken responsibility, resolved the situation.

Remember **YOU** need to show how **YOU** resolved the problem, you may have sought opinion or advice. But, **YOU** must have made the final decision to resolve the problem.

Consider word processing your answers first to check for spelling and grammar before writing your answers on a photocopied page to see if they will fit or can be expanded.

You can only make a maximum of 10 spelling, grammar, and punctuation mistakes before gaining a negative mark. Aim for no mistakes.

Check with the force you are applying to will accept a word processed application form. Many now do and a few are doing the initial application process online.

Core words or phrases to include in the answers include the following, "I identified", "I realised" and, "having spoken to him, I discovered that", "having identified the issue, I realised that one of my options was to...", "I decided", and so on. Notice that these are all "I" phrases and all of them demonstrate a sense of purpose and focus. The answer's need to be based around your response and your feelings, which are detailed and cover all the main points. Ensure your points are succinct and to the point. A larger space means a larger and more detailed answer. Try to utilise that space to explain your answer adding in key words/points. Stay gender and diverse neutral if appropriate. Remember that your answers will be graded, and that some forces may question you on the examples provided later on in the recruitment process. In addition, remember whilst everyone exaggerates slightly their involvement in certain incidents. If a force discovers you are blatantly lying, they will have serious doubts about your personal integrity, and any chance of recruitment will be lost. The key to success in this part of the form is to understand the purpose of the questions, and to spend some time finding the best example in your life experiences to illustrate the point required. Try to think of strong examples, as weaker examples tend to score more poorly. Many applicants simply write down a very brief and superficial experience, with no depth not bringing in key words or phrases. These lead to a low score and the application being rejected. Remember, 75% of applicants fail at the application stage due to poor examples and not answering the questions properly. It is essential that the answer is as thorough as possible.

As well as the four main competency questions there are another six questions asking.

Tell us why you want to become a police officer?

Tell us why you have applied to your chosen police force?

Tell us in some detail what tasks you expect to be undertaking as a police officer?
Tell us what effect you expect being a police officer to have on your social and domestic life?
What preparation have you undertaken before making this application to ensure that you know what to expect and that you are prepared for the role of police officer?
If you have previously applied to be a police officer, special constable or police community support officer (PCSO), what have you done since your last application to better prepare yourself for the role of a police officer?
These questions are also assessed so need to be well thought out and not just "I want to catch criminals" or "Going around with blue lights flashing". Think about the impact on your local community supporting the public and forging links as some ideas. Have you served as a special constable, PCSO, police cadets or been on a station visit/attended and open day or recruitment event. Do you live or work in the force you are applying to. Maybe you use to live there and understand the local community and want to make a difference. What about excellent customer service, which is very much what the college of policing and individual forces are looking for. A modern day police officer needs to be an excellent communicator, be understanding and empathetic to individuals, understand local communities and how these impact on local policing. On occasions they may need to problem solve, be it troublesome youths, parking issues, neighbourly disputes. In the current economic climate, this often needs to be done with no or very little spending. Making use of partner agencies, where possible or appropriate to solve issues. Remember that spelling, grammar and handwriting is still being assessed as are your responses. However, they are not graded the same as the four CBQs.

## *Special Constable Application Form*

The current application form for the Special Constabulary is now very similar to the full-time police officer application form. You may well find it quite long and arduous to fill out for a volunteer position. However, a Special Constable is now more than ever a professional member of the police family. When out on the streets the public sees a Special Constable the same as any other police officer, and expects the same high level of service and professionalism. Ensuring it is filled out correctly in black ink and readable will aid the recruitment process. The marking and standards of the application form, in terms of the competency assessment part of the application form are not expected to be as high.

The application form has two competency questions compared to the four on the full-time application form (Q1, Q2)

The last six questions are identical to the questions on the full-time application form just the word police officer replaced with special constable.

Q3 Tell us why you want to become a special constable?

Q4 Tell us why you have applied to your chosen police force?

Q5 Tell us in some detail what tasks you expect to be undertaken as a special constable?

Q6 Tell us what effect you expect being a special constable to have on your social and domestic life?

Q7 What preparation have you undertaken before making this application to ensure that you know what to expect and that you are prepared for the role of special constable?

Q8 If you have previously applied to be a police officer, special constable or police community support officer (PCSO), what have you done since your last application to better prepare yourself for the role of police officer?

They are looking for answers that show your rationale and commitment to becoming a special constable. Even though you are applying for a volunteer position treat it with just the same care and attention you would if you were applying for a paid position. For those looking to become a full-time officer later on it is also good practice!

### *PCSO Application Form*

The current application form for a PCSO is now very similar to the police constable application form. PCSOs are an important part of the police family and are a key element of the neighbourhood police teams. The role is ever expanding as PCSOs take on more and more of the role of a police officer. Some PCSOs now even carry handcuffs and can detain individuals for a set period of time. They are excellent at gathering low level intelligence bout the local area they work on. Ensuring it is filled out correctly in black ink and readable if the force you are applying to will not allow typeface, will aid the recruitment process. The marking and standards of the application form, in terms of the competency assessment part of the application form are not expected to be as high as police constable, but higher than special constable.

The application form has three competency questions compared to the four on the police constable application form (Q1, Q2, Q3)

Q4 Tell us why you want to become a police community support officer?

Q5On a day to day basis, what tasks do you expect to be carrying out as a police community support officer?

They are looking for answers that show your rationale and commitment to becoming a PCSO. Also your understanding of the role and the sorts of things you may do.

### *Competency Question Results*

You will receive the results of the competency assessment with feedback in the post. They come as an overall grade either A, B, C, or D. You need an overall grade B to pass or some forces require each of the four competencies assessed to be a B. You will receive feedback that is relative to the grade and the cohort that you applied with. The actual score is based on all the candidates that applied for the same application. This means you are competing against the other candidates rather than just a benchmark. It also explains why those that apply against internal applicants find their scores have dropped compared to when they applied with general applicants. Also, those that applied and passed the application form once, but failed the assessment centre, reapply and find the same answers do not pass a second time. Below, is a grade B and C result from the old seven competencies, but the feedback is similar with the new competencies as are the key improvements.
Here is an example of feedback for a Grade B answer.

Team Working: How you performed against other candidates: This performance met the overall standard required. You scored better than 58% of the candidates and only the top 4% candidates scored more highly than you. Candidates who achieved similar scores to you tended to demonstrate that they clearly understood the role they were playing within the team and evidenced clear co-operation between team members. Candidates that scored more highly than you demonstrated that they saw the outcomes as a team effort.
Here is an example of feedback for a Grade C answer.

Respect for Race and Diversity: How you performed against other candidates:
This performance met some of the requirements, however overall did not meet the standard required. Although you scored more highly than 25% of the candidates, 30% scored better than you. Candidates who achieved similar scores to you tended to use an example where the behaviour challenged was clearly insensitive, bullying or discriminatory. Candidates who scored higher than you evidenced that they directly challenged the behaviour and demonstrated they did so politely. You needed to provide evidence of challenging the behaviour and it was not enough if you dealt with the issue by addressing a group without the individual being clearly told. The evidence of challenging the behaviour had to be clear, and clear to the person who was a bully or discriminatory. If you did not demonstrate clearly telling the person what they had done was wrong, you will have scored less well.
The feedback is not that conclusive, but my tip is to look at the answers you scored higher in and the ones you did not score so highly in and look at why one question is better than the other. Often it will be due to the example used or possibly not enough of a story or key points missed.

# Assessment Centre

One of the most harrowing phase for any prospective police constable or PCSO applicant is the assessment day. The day will consist of a competency-based structured interview, tests, role plays and written exercises, which is made up of four questions. The assessment process takes around 5 hours for Police Constables and PCSOs and around 2-3 hours for Special Constables. At the end of the assessment centre you will feel quite drained and either unsure if you have passed or thinking you have failed. Most of those tend to feel they have done much worse than they actually have. It is deigned to be high pressured and intense. There has been occasions where some people have found it too much and walked out half way through the process. The individual tests themselves are not that challenging, when you know what to expect. However, the intensity and pressure of continuous assessment for nearly all of the 5 hours is. It is intentional to put you under pressure to see how you react under pressure. Go in with the thought, that it is a challenging assessment process, but one that is quite enjoyable and you WILL PASS. If you feel you have done badly on one section carry on putting in the effort, as you may not have done as badly as you think. Even if you have not got all the marks, you may well be able to do better on another part of the test. It is worth noting that only 5% of the total marks come from the numerical and verbal reasoning tests, which seem to worry more candidates than the actual role play element. The actual role plays are based around the Sergeant and Inspector role plays used for the police promotion exams. With a different and less complex scenario. They both work on a 5 minute preparation phase and 5 minute activity phase and similar marking, looking for you to show certain skills by how you interact and solve the role play. A tick is given for each element you demonstrate along with a score of between 1 and 5 for how well you demonstrated each of the competencies, that the particular role play was designed to cover. However, get a grade D in working with others and it is an automatic fail. The same in the written exercises, but not the structured interview. Along with the core competencies, you are also tested on your oral and written communication.

***The Four Parts of the Assessment Centre:***

Written exercise

There are two written exercises given as a scenario that is based on your role as a customer service advisor at a shopping centre. You need to give a handwritten solution to the problem. Each exercise lasts twenty minutes. You will be marked on the content – spelling, grammar, written communication, relevant score skill and respect for diversity.

Interactive exercise

You will be given preparatory information for five minutes before entering a room where there will be a role actor and an assessor present. You will take the role of a newly appointed customer services officer at a shopping centre. You will have five minutes to make a plan to the scenario you have been given and five minutes to deal with the problem/issue. This will be repeated four times. The assessors will mark you on how you deal with the issue, oral communication, respect for diversity, and relevant core skill.

Interview

You will be interviewed for a total of 20 minutes. There will be four questions and you will have five minutes to answer each question. You will be marked on oral communication, logical presentation of facts, relevant core skill and respect for diversity.

Police initial recruitment test

You will undertake two tests one is maths and the other verbal logic and reasoning.

### *What to Expect*

On arrival at the assessment centre, you will be put into a cohort of around 8 people usually from the same force that you are applying to. A cohort leader will guide you round each of the exercises in a set order, which varies between each of the four or five cohorts taking the test at the same time. Remember to watch what you say and do at ALL times. Say or do something that lacks diversity and you could be awarded a grade D for working with others leading to an automatic fail for the whole assessment.
You will get asked to sign a disclaimer at the end of the assessment centre. Asking you not to pass on the specifics of any of the exercises you have just undertaken, to ensure no one is given an unfair advantage. It is wise to say DON'T share your experience on social media as this could lead to a potential fail.
Whilst the sample exercises in this book and those that you can download from the College of Policing website are in a similar format. The ones in this book have been written as an example to aid in your preparation and an aid in your understanding of what may be asked of you.
All the exercises you will undertake, are to see how you compare to the core competencies. You are marked on what **YOU** did and what **YOU** said. The more competencies that can be marked off in theory the higher the score. Although you can also be marked down for showing negative competencies such as not showing understanding, won't work as a team, unable to follow instructions as some examples. It is in some ways a tick box exercise, as the assessors go through a list of competencies or indicators they expect to see in each section. Only the numerical and reasoning, multi choice tests are marked by a computer. At

the end of the day all the marks are fed into a computer to generate a score. Usually the results are sent directly to the force you are applying to within two weeks of the assessment centre. The feedback report and score will then be sent on to let you know if you have passed or failed. These days the reports are sent via email which does speed up the process of getting your results. As a rule of thumb the marking starts on the Friday after usual four assessment days have been run, depending on demand. They then have 10 working days to mark and get the results back to the force you are applying for. An example of an assessment report is in the Appendix at the back of the book.

Anyone wishing to join the Police Service of England and Wales as a full-time police constable must attend the Police SEARCH® Recruit assessment centre at the College of Policing. Less the British Transport Police who have their own assessment process. PCSOs now also attend an assessment day, but like on the application form the overall score they require is lower and there are less role plays (two instead of four).

Once you have been successful on the application form and passed the required standard for the CBQs. The force you are applying to will write or email to say you have passed the CBQs, usually at the same time giving a date for your assessment centre. You must be given a minimum of two weeks notice for the assessment centre.

The Assessment Centre assessors evaluate candidates' performance in exercises related to core competencies. Information from all of the exercises is used to produce the final results. They give you at least three chances at the six competencies and average your grade out for each of the six competencies. However, Working with others is assessed in every exercise and you need to score at least 50% to pass overall.

Assessment exercises for a police constable include:

A competency-based interview with 4 questions lasting 20 minutes in total
A numerical reasoning test lasting 12 minutes
A verbal, logical reasoning test lasting 25 minutes
Two written exercises lasting 20 minutes each
Four interactive exercises lasting 10 minutes each.
All candidates undertake the same exercises and are assessed on an equal basis. The assessment centre lasts approximately half a day or about five hours.

### *Assessment Day Scoring*

Grades are awarded at the assessment centre based on what you did and how well you did it. These grades are then converted into numbers (A=3, B=2, C=1, D=0). In order to have met the national standard at the assessment centre candidates must score 50% overall. This score is derived from your performance in all six competencies assessed as well as Written Communication and Oral Communication.
In addition to obtaining a 50% score overall you must also score 50% in Working with Others, 50% in Oral Communication and 44% in Written Communication. It is therefore possible to score more than 50% overall, but have not met the national standard by scoring less than the required mark in one or more of the other areas.
The assessment centre, national pass grade is currently 50% for a police officer and you must pass working with others, otherwise you will fail the whole assessment. Quite a few forces now require a pass grade of 60%. All elements carry a minimum national standard of 50% less written communication, which requires a minimum of 44% to pass. The grading is ABC and D and you are looking to get an overall average grade of a C. However, even if you average a B but get a D in working with others you will still

fail the assessment centre. Overall in an assessment centre there are 123 marks available. If you achieved 50% overall this means you obtained 1/2 of the 123 marks available. If you scored 60% you obtained 73 marks.
For working with others there are a total of 21 marks available. If you scored 52% this equates to 11 out of the 21 marks. 57% equates to 12 marks.
In Oral Communications there are a total of 15 marks available. If you obtained 87% this means you scored 13 out of the 15 marks available.
For Written Communications there are just 9 marks available. If you scored 33%, this means you scored just 3 out of the 9 marks. Even if you obtained 100% in working with others, decision making, this only accounts for 45 marks out of the 123. So although you may have met the required standard for these 3 competency areas, it is still possible you are rejected because your overall score did not meet the requirement. The remaining 78 marks are accounted for in professionalism, decision making, openness to change, service delivery, and public service. So if you scored:
49% Overall
90% Working with others
100% Oral communications
100% Service delivery
This means you scored 60 marks out of 123 overall. 19 out of 21 marks for working with others, 15 marks out of 15 marks for Oral Communications and 9 marks out of 9 for service delivery. Because you only achieved 60 marks overall (49%), this standard is not sufficient to join any force. As a rule of thumb thinking back to the core competency positive indicators you get a mark for each positive competency you show and potentially lose a mark for each negative competency you show. Having a good

working knowledge of the competencies and knowing the keywords will help you to score better. Also remember to not show any negative indicators so you don't lose marks.

In order of importance the most marks are awarded to the role play (57%) followed by written exercises (26%), structured interview (12%) and finally the IQ tests (5%). If you gain a D on either the written or interactive phase in working with others it is an automatic fail. You can still pass, however, if you gain a D in the structured interview.

For each section less the IQ, you are marked for each skill within a competency you show on a pre written marking sheet, along with a strength grade between 1 and 5 or A to D. The strength grades usually have a heading based one of the six competencies that are being assessed in that particular role play/written exercise/structured interview. The actual marking sheet in the role plays, for example, is simply a list with tick boxes and then several 1 to 5 grades at the bottom covering several of the competencies. The ticks in a generalised form may be for:

Did you apologise?

Did you ask what the issue was?

Did you identify the problem?

Did you challenge a particular comment?

Did you come up with a solution?

Did you ask if the customer/staff/shop owner as happy?

Did you summarise the problem/complaint?

Again, these are not an actual example, more a generalisation as they are specific for each role play, written exercise or structured interview element being covered. Therefore, looking at the scoring it is easy to see that the most important element is the role plays, followed by the written exercise. The English and maths tests that more people seem to worry about than the role play only carry 5% of the marks. The role plays should be your

main focus for preparation. These are also what most people have very little experience of and lose the most marks on. The written exercises are quite straightforward, as long as you state the problem and provide a viable and justifiable solution. Written in a concise manner, with preferably no, spelling, grammar or punctuation mistakes. If your handwriting is hard to read, consider printing, practice writing a letter about poor service you may have received with an introduction (outline problem), middle (how the problem affected you and what you want to be done about it) and finally a conclusion (summarise your letter saying what would make you happy).
In the interactive and written exercises, you may play the part of a newly appointed customer-services officer at a retail and leisure complex called The Westshire Centre. The Westshire Centre is a made up place created for the assessment centre only. There are other scenarios that have been used before such as a leisure centre. All the scenarios are looking at your customer service and problem solving skills against the six Skills for Justice Competencies. They are looking at how you deal with various situations in particular diversity issues and effective communication skills. But the scenarios will also bring in resilience, customer service skills, problem solving and maybe team working. Many people use to fall down on diversity with 30% failing the assessment centre on diversity. Whilst the new six skills do not have a unique diversity skill. However, in **professionalism** it does state unacceptable behaviour and challenging it, which would include diversity. This is why knowing the content of the six competencies to aid you in either stating keywords or simply ensuring you demonstrate that skill, to gain another tick.
The four interactive exercises are based around putting you into situations with actors to see how you react. You have five

minutes to plan and set and a further five minute activity phase to deal with the scenario with an actor who is either an ex-police officer or civilian staff but not a professional actor.
Any scenario will have been tried and tested lots of times before you undertake it so you will be able to resolve the issues in the five minutes you have. The scenario may be dealing with an underperforming member of staff. A complaint from the member of the public about the facilities or another member of staff. The key points to be successful, I will outline below after I have talked about another crucial element '**planning**'.
You will be provided with essential information in the form of memo/email/letter of complaint and they will give you a big hint on what the scenario will be about to aid in the planning. So many applicants forget or do not plan what they are going to do in the scenario. Under the pressure of the moment become flustered and lose valuable marks by missing out key points or elements. Planning is essential and the easiest method I have seen to plan is to use the CAR (Circumstance Action Result) method. You can then take that plan into the roleplay, you won't be able to add any more notes in the actual role play. Any notes are not marked or form part of the assessment, but are crucial if you want a high score. They will give your role play structure and key points, to aid in asking questions and planning a response. They will ensure you do not miss any key points or questions. Even making use of existing documentation to provide a response. It is also important to reiterate that with only 5 minutes in the activity phase, none of the issues will be overly complex. The supplied background materials will outline half of the issue with the other half requiring you to fill in the gap by asking questions. Before then offering an appropriate solution, the roleplayer will NEVER give you a solution and don't waste time asking. Maybe ask if they are happy or what they would like doing, but don't try to

persuade them to pick a preferred option. You are being assessed if you can make a decision and follow it through even if challenged. Ask a question that they cannot answer the role play actor will bow their head – look for this block and ask another question! When you ask them what they would like doing (this is an essential question and part of good customer care). They may want an individual sacking, but that is not really an ethical solution, without further investigation and proven to be the only option, which it never is, in the role play scenarios. Is firing someone good customer service all round. It may be for the customer, but what about the company you work for, the individual who will be sacked? A written warning or action plan are much more appropriate actions in the role play scenarios. Remember, you are not fully in the real world, whilst the scenarios are designed to be realistic, you would not expect a customer service officer to solve an employee or customer issue in 5 minutes after having only 5 minutes to plan, hence re-iterating that the scenarios are all pretty straightforward. Don't 'overthink' or come up with weird and wonderful solutions. Question, verify, challenge, explain consequences, and provide a solution (where appropriate).

The **CAR** system has three elements:

**Circumstances** – What important/key details have you been given, look for anything that is a diversity issue and you may need to challenge. Any challenges need to be polite and explain why you think what they have said or written is unacceptable.

**Action –** What are you going to do, maybe list questions you will ask or points you need clarifying. It is highly unlikely that you will be able to resolve the issue without asking questions. Clarify any points to aid in formulating a plan.

**Results** – What are you going to do to resolve the situation, maybe list a few options or action points for each element?

Summarise the key points and ask if the individual happy with your response.
The best way to structure CAR is on the plain sheet of paper you will be provided with, spilt it up into three parts, then put the CAR headings in each section and then work through each section in the five minutes you have. Bullet points is the simplest method as they are structured and easy to work through logically. A page of notes may be comprehensive, but you may miss out elements or struggle to find the key point you wanted to address or cover. Don't worry if you are unsure which element should go where using CAR. The essential element is to plan and have a structure to work from. Insert important key words from the supplied materials that need further questioning. Reminders to say sorry if required, ask if they are happy, specific questions. Anything that will aid you in the activity phase. Fail to plan is planning to fail and you will almost certainly miss key points. Remember the supplied information is all there for a reason, never overlook any of it. Again by planning if the role play actor says something you were not expecting you can deal with it and move back onto your plan. One of the main the differences between a strong and weak candidate in the role plays is having a structure. Below is an example structure to either memorise or to write down. Even a simple step like writing at the top of the page if it is an employee, customer or shop owner, you are dealing with, may help if you go blank or as a prompt.
STEP 1
Introduce yourself to the role actor and ask him/her how you can help them. You may find that the role actor starts talking the minute you walk in the room. Don't be put off just say OK, tell them you will take a seat. Before going through your introduction. Rehearse a version that you can use in each role

play. As the basic introduction, to a customer, shop owner or employee will be the same.

(Remember to be polite and treat the role play actor in a sensitive and supportive manner. You are being assessed against the core competency of working with others during every role play scenario).

STEP 2

Listen to them carefully and ask relevant questions to establish the facts.

(How, When, Where, Why, Who).

STEP 3

Clarify the information received to check you have understood exactly what has happened. If a customer or shop owner, ask them what they would like you to do about their issue.

STEP 4

Provide a suitable solution to the problem or situation and tell the role play actor what you intend to do. Refer to any policy documents to justify your decision where appropriate. If further investigation or follow up meeting required, state YOU will take personal responsibility for the investigation / meeting.

STEP 5

Check to confirm that the role play actor is happy with your solution. (They may not be, but follow through with your decision if it is ethically and morally right).

If time allows, provide a final summary of what you intend to do and ask them if there is anything else you can help them with.

***Role Play Preparation Template***

Customer/employee/shop owner

Name of Role Play

Good morning/afternoon, please take a seat

(if standing)

My name is… Customer Service Officer
Thank you for the letter /coming to meeting (apologise if manager cannot be present)
Outline issue, apologise if appropriate
First question (write out verbatim)
Answer- Probe further or challenge as inappropriate comment?
Second question
Answer- probe further or challenge as inappropriate comment?
Extra questions as required depending on the scenario
What would they like doing about the issue if appropriate
Challenge any equality issues – refer to equality policy
Solution – What are you going to do to resolve problem.
Are they happy?
Summarise
Anything else I can do for you today?

### *Some key points for the role playing element*

The information you need in the preparation phases of the exercises will be supplied and as part of your assessment day invitation, you will be given a detailed overview of the scenario as part of the information pack. You will also find a copy of the information usually on the seat in the Scenario room. It is important to read and understand all the information fully. The interactive exercises will have you dealing with various situations based on the six competencies and you are then graded on how you resolve and react to each situation. A buzzer system is used to denote the start of your preparation time and interactive phase. Actors in the scenario play various customers and employees. These actors are a mixture of police staff and retired police officers, they are not trained actors. They can and do make mistakes, try to ignore a mistake and carry on with your plan. Be polite and treat them as an information tool that you need to interact with. The way they lower their heads at the end of the role play and start talking to you the moment you walk through the door, does seem  little surreal. Again, remember this is not a real scenario and is designed to test you and see how you perform. Just be polite and stick to your plan, asking questions to ensure you solve the issue.

The current scenario is built around a shopping centre and your role as a customer service officer. You will be supplied with pre-read material, which covers the job description of a customer services officer, along with facilities, rules and most importantly an equality statement. If you learn the basic outline and are familiar with the job role and the basics of the shopping centre, this will save valuable time during both the role plays and written exercises. How to challenge discriminatory behaviour is an important element. It involves three steps that will come up in at least one of the scenarios, so knowing this cannot be overstated.

Any person who believes that a member of staff is discriminating against or harassing a colleague or customer should take action as quickly as possible. We recommend doing the following:

a) Ask the person to stop. (In some cases, people may not be aware of the effects of their behaviour.)

b) Discuss the problem with an appropriate person. If you are not sure about what to do, whether the behaviour could be classed as discrimination or harassment, or whether you should make a complaint, you can get advice from a Customer Services Officer or your manager.

c) Make a formal complaint. You can complain in writing to the Centre Manager.

The Centre Manager will then investigate your complaint and take appropriate action.

In total you will undertake 4 role plays for police constable or two for PCSO, each one you get 5 minutes preparation time and 5 minutes to undertake the role play. Any materials, that you are given are there for a reason, so don't dismiss, as they most likely form part of the role play. Remember **CAR** and plan, with bullet points, to aid you. Never argue or raise your voice, stay as calm as collected as you can in what some find is quite difficult under pressure. Always sit down and work through your pre-prepared plan, try not to get flustered and just keep asking relevant questions.

I have given a role play example below and there are more at the end of the book to practice with. Note that the name of the exercise relates to the person's surname and could be either male or female. None of the role plays are really hard, however you will need to ask questions and use the supplied information to get the full picture and give a resolution that **YOU** have come up with, just like a police officer would have to. A role player may be angry at first, but cannot stay angry as you would not complete the role play. Their responses are limited by the role play, so asking questions outside of the role play will not be answered and waste time. Look for hooks, i.e. vague elements that require further questions. Put a bullet point into your CAR plan, reminding you to ask the role play actor to expand or explain the comment. Don't bother with small talk, be polite and friendly, but idle chit chat, will not score any marks. If you finish within the five minutes, ask if they are happy with the outcome, re-cap the problem and/or solution. If you have made an ethical decision that fits in with the shopping centre's policies, stand by your decision even if it is unpopular. The types of scenarios are quite varied and can be quite topical some current ones have been:

A person refusing to remove a hat and asking why wearing a Burqa or Turban is acceptable, but they cannot wear a hat whilst in the centre.

A man complaining about gypsies using the centre and causing trouble.
A lady has been injured by a security guard, as the security barged past trying to catch someone who has just stolen a mobile phone.
Groups of youths are constantly congregating outside a shop, putting off customers
A member of staff using a computer to do their own shopping in work time and have suddenly started to underperform.
Youths skateboarding and smoking in the centre
Security guard making an unacceptable remark
Important points to remember:
Understand the six skills and you will see how these fit in with the scenario. Remember working with others is part of every scenario. Be understanding, empathetic whilst not showing any bias to one party over another.

Remember, you are a customer service officer and behave as one, or how you would expect one to behave in a leisure centre or shopping centre. Never try to approach the scenarios as if you are a police officer or use police jargon. Be polite and non-aggressive at all times.

If a role player makes a comment, be it  welfare issue or needs to be challenged, it is natural to say 'oh dear' or instantly challenge, just say OK, pause and then either challenge if inappropriate of if a staff welfare issue you may now have a reason for their poor performance.
Plan, plan, plan, I cannot overstate how important it is to use the preparation time to pull out key points and place in an ordered bullet point list. Read quickly and read everything, unless the information is part of the pre-read, which you should already have learnt.

Add your greeting and first question verbatim to your plan. Having the first part to reel off will set you up for a good start and will prevent nerves making you go blank. The minute you reel off your first question, your nerves will disappear and you will move forward with the role play.

Never assume a name you have been given is male or female.

Challenge any diversity issues either said or written in a polite manner explaining why. They may well be quite subtle, remember this is the police standard of diversity not your own. If you are given a policy relating to the roleplay, reference it, read out the first sentence or element that sums up in one sentence. Remember a policy that has been provided as part of the preparation material is there for a reason!

Odd scenarios start with an angry customer/staff member, stay calm they will have been told to only be angry for a set time. Stay calm, allow them to finish before asking them to sit down "would you like to take a seat". Stay polite and explain the issue in a rational way. They may not calm down instantly, but don't be put off, continue with your plan and remain calm and polite.
You are watched and observed to see how you behave and interact even with other candidates. Expect the unexpected and be aware at all times during the day. Never mention anything about any of the role plays to other candidates during the actual assessment day.

Remember the assessors are looking for **YOU** to solve the problem. Good ideas are a letter of apology, meeting that you will personally chair, and training opportunities. Think of ideas that are cost effective. No point saying you will put in 1,000 CCTV cameras and 200 hundred security guards as that would be unrealistic.

Make sure, you question and probe to get all the information. If an employee, maybe look at welfare issues, lack of training, unaware of a policy, if a customer find out why they have that particular opinion. You will need to ask questions to get the information needed to give a resolution. Fail to question and you will fail the role play.

Look for pointers in the scenario material and formulate questions or potential references to the pre read material, you were sent before attending the assessment centre. Learn and understand the policies such as the Equality and code of conduct policy given in the pre-read. Both **WILL** be used during your assessment, in both the role plays and written exercises.
Don't make any assumptions; an underperforming member of staff for example, may have reasons such as problems at home. A customer may have been given the wrong information. An employer may not have been rude, they may have simply challenged a racist remark made by a customer.

You will need to make a decision on what to do; the actor will not make the decision for you. The assessors are looking at you to be decisive as part of the core competencies. Then follow through with your decision, even when challenged.

Try to keep to a timing schedule of one minute for the initial introduction to the problem, two-three minutes discussing the problem and questioning. Finally the last minute discussing your solution to the problem.

Ask what they would like to be done, ask the role player if they are happy with the outcome. Whilst they may not give you an answer or even an unrealistic answer like "they should be sacked." You have shown to be considering their views and offering a high level of customer service by including their thoughts and views.

Each role play will seem to go very quick and you will feel quite drained, have a plan, understand the six competencies and ensure no diversity opportunities are missed. Then your chances of getting the marks needed to pass the day will be greatly improved.

Remember that you need to constantly offer a high level of customer service, what does a high level of customer service mean to you?

Finally, don't panic, remember 5 minutes is not very long to question and solve an issue. The scenarios are designed to be relatively simple and for the average candidate to be able to complete. Some scenarios may require you to **personally** investigate further, which in turn may actually be the final solution!

### *Role Play Example*

In this exercise you have been given three pieces of information in the preparation phase.

- A memo from Pete Green, Operations Manager
- A letter from Clancy, Customer at the Centre
- A copy of The Northshire Centre Positive Action Statement

In this exercise you will meet Clancy

Memo

**To:** Customer Services Officer

**From:** Pete Green, Operations Manager
**Re:** Complaint from Customer

I have just received a letter of complaint from Clancy a customer at the centre.
I attached a copy of the letter of complaint for your perusal.
Clancy wishes to complain about a vendor located on the ground floor of the centre. The vendor concerned has been identified as Ms Singh the owner of tongs and twirls, a hair products supplier.

We have monitored Ms Singh and thus far have not identified any wrongdoing; in fact, her and her team appear to be well received in the centre by staff and visitors. I had arranged for Clancy to meet me today, however, I now have to attend an urgent health and safety meeting. Can you please meet with Clancy and progress the matter?
Regards
Pete Green
Pete Green
Operations Manager
Operations Manager
The Northshire Centre
North Road
Northshire
NR12 5PN

Dear Operations Manager,

After visiting the Northshire Centre this morning I felt I had to write to complain about the actions of one of the vendors in the centre. I frequently visit your centre every Tuesday without any

issues or problems. However, recently a new vendor has appeared on the ground floor and has been causing me some difficulties. This morning, as I was walking past the vendor they were rude to me. This is not the first time this has happened either. I have seen their type on many occasions be rude to other shoppers. Something needs to be done about this matter, or I shall have to consider taking my custom elsewhere.
Yours faithfully
Clancy
Northshire Equality Policy
It is the policy of The Stamford Centre that no person shall be treated less or more favourable on the grounds of political opinion, gender, marital status, religion, race, sexual orientation or disability. The centre, particularly welcomes individuals and staff from these backgrounds, as they are currently under-represented in the centre. The centre does not tolerate harassment or prejudice on any grounds. We consider such matters as serious and we may consider reporting such incidents to the police. It is the responsibility of staff and centre users to abide by this policy as it supports the centre on positive action matters. However, should a member of staff or centre user behave in a prejudice manner or cause harassment, they should be dealt with.
The following action should be taken:
**a)** Approach the person, discuss their behaviour and then ask them politely to refrain from behaving in any manner not consistent with the beliefs and values of this policy.
(Be mindful when discussing the matter, that some people may simply not be aware
of the impact their actions or behaviour).
**b)** Make the Centre Manager aware of the incident.
**c)** Staff should record such matters in the Incident Report book.

**d)** Victims are encouraged to make a formal written complaint to the Centre Manager.

The Centre Manager will then investigate the matter and take appropriate action.

All matters will be dealt with in confidence.

In the first 5 minutes of the planning phase, go through the supplied pieces of information and pull out the key points. By virtue of the fact that a copy of the positive action statement has been included, a strong candidate will know there will be an issue around this. The letter and the memo from the manager have conflicting information, again this should point out the need to question Clancy about what has happened and why they felt the way they did. Bullet point all key points and questions using the CAR method, reference this in the 5 minute activity phase to help you structure, as you will feel under pressure. Making it all too easy to get flustered and forget or drift off, potentially loosing you marks. Below is an example structure, by changing the bits in bold you can use it for all four of the role plays, helping to make preparation for each role play much easier.

Meet and greet, stating who you are and job role, then ask the person to sit down in a polite manner if they are not already seated.

Thank them for their letter/attending meeting and apologise for the manager not being present.

Summarise issue/problem

Point out any positive points that you have drawn out from the materials

Ask questions - what did the vendor say to make them think they were rude?

What do they mean - **by their type?**

Challenge any diversity issues – reference equality policy

Explain the vendor has been monitored and no issues found

Offer to personally investigate the matter further
Offer to personally keep Clancy updated
Ask if they are happy with your suggestions
If challenged, stand by your decision as being the ethical and right thing to do
Summarise all your points
Anything else you can do for them

### *Assessment Day Structured Interview*

The assessment day interview will last for up to 20 minutes and you will be asked four questions about how you have dealt with specific situations in the past. These questions will be related to the six competencies. You will be given up to five minutes to answer each of the four questions. The person interviewing you will stop you if you go over the five minutes. As the person interviewing you asks you the question, they will also give you a copy of the question to refer to. They may ask you further questions to help you to give a full response. When you consider your responses to the interview questions, only choose examples that you feel comfortable discussing with the person interviewing you. It is well worth thinking of examples of the six competencies before you attend your assessment day. You can use the ones you used on your application form if they scored well or think of new ones. It is always a good idea to have at least two examples for each competency. Working with others will always be one of the questions. Trying to answer these off the cuff will prove to be quite difficult, and reduce your chances of scoring quite so well. It is also all too easy to become flustered or forgetful under pressure.

As each of the questions relate to one of the six competencies you already have a chance to formulate potential answers. Then to make life even easier on the pre-read material you will receive before the assessment centre, it will state the four competencies that questions will be based on. Allowing you time, to think of an example and prepare. There are not many interviews where you get to see the questions before an interview! You may even be able to use the examples from the CBQs you undertook on your application form. Just be prepared to be quizzed further, and if these have just been made up you may struggle to expand on your answers or falter under scrutiny.

You will be given each of the questions on a laminated sheet to refer to for each question. The interviewer will not give you any sense on how you are doing. They are trained not to smile or make any acknowledgment of what you have just said. After a couple of minute's pause for the interviewer to ask another question. After 5 minutes they will move onto the next question regardless if you have finished or not. If you have rehearsed each answer well, it will be pretty straightforward and the extra questions will just expand on a particular element. Like "how did you overcome the difficulties…" "What did you do to…?" Very similar questions to the ones on the initial application form. As a best practice, have at least two examples for each of the four competency's being covered in the interview. Working with others will most certainly be one of the four competencies being covered.

At the start of your interview you will be lined up outside a door and told when you can knock and enter.

### *Written Exercises*

The written exercises are very much like the 10-minute role play exercises, in that you have to read through the information and then deliver a solution. In the case of the written exercises, it is in the form of a letter or memo as opposed to an actor. The written exercises are pass or fail. For the written exercise, you have 20

minutes to plan and then write a response. Just like the role play exercises use the CAR method and spend only five minutes on the planning, leaving 15 minutes to write a neat and error free letter. You will be graded on punctuation, spelling and grammar. Write neatly and at a pace that enables the least amount of mistakes, but still conveys all the information you need to get across. If you come across a word you cannot spell, then think of another suitable word. Again, make sure any diversity issues are addressed in your response.
Since August 2015 police forces have had a choice on how they want written communication to be assessed. They now have four options in how they assess written communication. Which one is used will be stated during the initial application process.

Complete two written exercises completed before the assessment centre –candidates would need to pass the written exercises to attend the Police Recruitment Assessment Centre.

Complete two written exercises during the assessment centre – candidates would need to pass this written exercises in order to be successful at the assessment centre.

Accept a qualification of written English before the assessment centre –forces may ask candidates to complete a specific qualification, or provide evidence of having completed a specific qualification before they are able to attend the Police Recruitment Assessment Centre. The qualification can be at the police force's discretion, but must be at a minimum level of Functional Skills Level 2 English (or equivalent).

Accept a qualification of written English obtained after the assessment centre. A police force may ask candidates to complete or provide evidence of having completed a specific qualification after they have attended the assessment centre. Candidates must have completed the qualification prior to being signed off as a Police Constable.

Presently nearly all police forces are opting for the written communication to be assessed at the assessment centre.
Along with the four options the actual written exercise were changed in both the actual exercises and how the information required to write the report was given to the candidate. These exercises are the same if they are completed either before or during the assessment centre. Both exercises last for 30 minutes and are conducted in an exercise room with all the other candidates in your group. At the start of the exercise a briefing is giving in what is going to happen. All pens and paper are provided. You are allowed to take notes to aid with the written response.
The skills being tested is your ability to comprehend and summarise information accurately, structure responses logically and to use spelling and grammar correctly. The two new exercises consist of a set of typed instructions that you will use to write and incident report. The second exercise you will view a DVD which depicting an individual being interviewed. You will take notes and then use these notes to write an incident report from what you have seen.
Remember these exercises will not be vast and complex as there is simply not the time. They will be quite simple for the average recruit to resolve. You need to look for all the problematic issues and resolve them, and also any diversity comment that needs challenging. Ensure you give a reason for your suggested solution. This is where having a good working knowledge of the six competencies really helps and will pay dividends when

formulating your response. Even use the odd key word, just like you may have done on your CBQs within the application form. As well as the ability to communicate in writing, you are being assessed on your ability to understand and summarise information, see both sides of the problem, make a decision, generate creative solutions, evaluate solutions and finally convey that solution with a rationale.

For the written exercise, you should really start with a short introduction outlining the issues. Then follow on with how you intend to resolve these issues. Finally, challenge any diversity issues and a short conclusion. The key part here is to structure your response and make full use of the notes you have written.It is important to be concise but still write in full sentences. Think about what competencies are being assessed, and tailor your answer towards them. Don't feel you have to remember or throw in key words, just be mindful of what the assessors are looking for. It is undoubtedly going to be written communication, working with others, decision making, and service delivery. But may also be professionalism and public service. Hence, why having a good working understanding of the six competencies will aid the whole assessment process. In some ways the written exercises are easier to deal with than the role plays. The scenarios, however, tend to be slightly more complex.

Outline and summarise the issue. Only use facts from what you have been given or seen. Don't make assumptions or assume the individual is guilty unless the facts say so.

Write a conclusion summarising the incident. Ensure spelling, grammar and punctuation are correct. Only use words you can spell and write neatly.

Don't use jargon but do weave in any key words from the core competencies where appropriate.

Your wrist will ache from both the amount of writing. However, ensure what you have written is neat and legible. The two written exercises are virtually back to back, but for a strong, well prepared candidate, it provides a good opportunity to score well.

Make good use of your notes and ensure key points of the incident are recorded. A description of the person in the interview is a good idea. Start with an outline of the incident if possible.

Remember about good time management, don't spend more than 5 minutes reading the information, before beginning to write, otherwise you WILL run out of time.

Remember, nearly a third of the assessment centre marks come from the two written exercises. You have enough time to score highly by being succinct and showing you have gathered all the necessary information for the written instructions and DVD.

### *PIRT/Psychometric tests*

At the Assessment centre you will undertake two separate tests which will involve three papers one maths and two verbal logic and reasoning test in one book. Special Constables may also undertake similar tests at their local force as opposed to an assessment centre.

1. Numerical reasoning – this lasts 12 minutes and involves basic maths.

2. Verbal logical reasoning – this lasts 25 minutes involves being given a situation that you have to evaluate to decide if it is true, false or impossible to say.

There are some examples at the end of the book to give you an idea of what is expected. One of the best tips is not to try to complete all the answers, but to choose answers that you can give quickly and under pressure. If you find any difficulties then move onto the next question. Then re-visit any you have failed to complete. During the maths test at the assessment centre, you will be provided with a calculator.

The PIRT test consists of several skill areas.

*Verbal Usage Test* – the ability to spell words and construct sentences accurately.

*Checking Information* – the ability to check information quickly and correctly.

***Working with Numbers*** – the ability to solve numerical problems accurately.

***Verbal Reasoning*** – the ability to reason logically when given facts about events.

Note that the highlighted tests are the ones used at the assessment centre. The new tests being used by some forces consist of a numerical reasoning test, which will ask you to answer multiple-choice questions that will measure your ability to solve number problems accurately. At the assessment centre you will be provided with a calculator. Also a verbal, logical and reasoning test where you will asked to answer multiple-choice questions which will measure your ability to make logical sense of a situation when you are given facts about it.

### *What Can You do to Give Your Best Performance?*

Don't be down-hearted if you find the questions difficult or get a lot of them wrong. There are many things you can do to improve your performance. Practice is one answer, another is to simply slow down and take your time. The tests are not designed for you to be able to completely finish them. It merely assesses that you can undertake tasks efficiently and to a set standard.

Practice doing simple arithmetic without using a calculator. Do number puzzles. Do the scoring when playing games such as darts, card games. Put a ruler or something similar with a straight edge under lists. Take a few deep breaths before you start and don't try to rush.

Make sure that you know what you have to do before you start putting pencil to paper – if you do not understand, ask the person who is administering the test.

Read the instructions carefully before each test starts in order to make sure that you understand. Don't skim through them – you may overlook important details and in consequence make mistakes you could have avoided.

Even if you have taken the test before, don't assume that the instructions (and the worked examples) are the same as the last time – they may have changed.

Once the test begins work as quickly and as accurately as you can. Choose an easy to answer question first to boost confidence. Avoid spending too much time on questions you find difficult. Find an easier question then go back later if you have time. If you are uncertain about an answer, enter your best reasoned choice (but avoid simply guessing).
If you have some spare time after you have answered all questions, go back and check through your answers.

Keep working as hard as you can throughout the test – the more correct answers you get the higher your score will be.
Be positive in your attitude. Previous failures in tests or examinations are in the past and you should not allow that to have a detrimental effect on your performance on this occasion. Focus and believe you can pass the test.

### *Recruitment process summary*

During the whole application process where most candidates fall short is the lack of preparation. You really need to understand the role that you are applying for and then be able to convey your understanding of this to the recruitment staff. Understanding what a police officer actually does along with the core competencies is the first step. For example, during the final interview you are likely to receive a question similar to the following: "please describe a situation where you have to work as a team, what was the outcome and what role did you play in this. Now, while this question is obviously referring to the core competency of working with others, an essential requirement if you want to become a police officer, other questions are not so simple to determine what core competency you are required to demonstrate. However, if you do not know these core competencies off by heart you will not be able to work out how you should be answering the question and this will not score you high marks.
Referring back to the question above, if you have not thought about a time in your life where you have been able to work as a team it is quite difficult for most people to think about this right there and then. So what starts to happen is panic sets in and you cannot think clearly. Then the answer you give is the first example that comes to mind even if it does not quite meet what is being asked for. However, it is only later when you leave the interview

do you think “I should of said that" or "why didn't I use that example" and the reason for this is that you are now in a calm and relaxed manner.

A strong candidate will have a couple of examples that they have given considerable thought to before attending the assessment centre, so that even if the question doesn't match exactly, they can simply adapt their answer to meet the specific core competency that is being tested. Better still, try to have examples for each of the core competencies. You will have given four on your application form so think of ones for the remaining two. Always pause and give a few second to absorb the question and start to formulate a reply before actually answering it.

Some candidates may think that as long as they give a good example, why does it matter if they give the correct core competency? The answer to this question is firstly is shows that you do not understand what is being asked from you and secondly that you have failed to prepare for this role. The recruitment staff are, looking, for people who have taken their application seriously and given considerable thought to their recruitment. Remember these recruiters have seen many different types of candidates and will have a skill for detecting those that know what they are talking about and have prepared. Whilst on one hand you are not supposed to need to prepare for the assessment, other than reading the welcome pack and SEARCH assessment centre information. Preparation is the key to being successful starting with understanding the competencies, remembering the key points in the welcome pack, think about what exceptional customer service is.

So as well as preparing a list of examples for particular situations that you can recall and adapt to give specific and related answers the other part of the application process you need to prepare for is the police role play. While many candidates want to be part of the everyday environment that a police officer experiences, very few will have actually experienced this in real life. The role play scenarios will access your abilities to deal with certain situations, your manner and how you apply yourself. In the end they want to see how many of the core competency indicators you can match. The more positive indicators you match the higher your score and in theory overall grade.

### *Fitness Test*

The fitness test is usually taken at the force you are applying to. The idea of the test is to test your endurance and dynamic strength. The dynamic test involves performing five seated chest pushes and five seated back pulls on the dyno machine to measure your strength. The standard is 35Kg pushing and pulling on the dyno machine.

The second part is the endurance part where you will be asked to run to and fro along a 15 metre track in time with a series of bleeps, which become increasingly faster. The pass level is 5.4 on the bleep test. It is not as nearly as bad as it sounds, the actual test lasting 3 ½ minutes or 44 lengths. The key is to just keep with the bleeps, the odd Gazelle will race ahead at the speed of sound. But, if you have never done it before, pace yourself and just stay with the beeps. You will undertake the same endurance test as part of your fitness to be an operational police officer. I was worried the first time I undertook it and did pace myself the second time I knew could go a little faster knowing what to expect! The tip here is set up a practice test and try doing 44, 15 metre lengths in 3 ½ minutes. It is also important to remember you are competing against a set standard not each other.

If you do not pass on the first attempt. Talk to the fitness instructor for a training plan to get you up to speed. Also, be aware of your weight and that your BMI (Body Mass Index)

needs to be below 30. You can retake your fitness test up to three times – better still start getting your fitness built up slowly now, even with longer more brisk walks. You could also cycle, swim or jog.
The police fitness test is not that hard as you are not applying to the SAS. It is no problem for a person with average fitness and of all ages people in their 40s and 50s pass the bleep test as part of their annual fitness test routinely.

### *The Final Interview*

The final force interview if your chosen force does a final interview. Is where you get a chance to be yourself and also ask questions as well as questions being asked of you. You may well be asked why you want to be a police officer and your career aspirations. Try not to use the usual, "To fight crime" it should be more about supporting your local community and making a difference within the community. Remember being a police interview, the questions will be competency based, so take a few seconds to think of a good example before answering the question. It is a good idea to revise and understand the area of the force you are applying to join. What is their mission statement and force priorities. Look at a recent HMIC report to find out the challenges the force faces, as well as what they do well and not quite so well.
There are nearly always questions about 'Force Priorities' and the current and future force plan. You may be asked who the Crime Commissioner. Their website may also have the force priorities as a downloadable document or webpage. If so READ it and understand what types of crime and possible funding solutions the force is focusing on. The more you can learn about your chosen force, the more confident you will feel answering questions about the force. The new College of Policing Code of

Ethics available on their website, will help you understand further the expectations of a police officer.
Don't forget, being a Police Officer is now very much community and customer focused. It is important to treat people as individuals with respect and dignity. It is almost a certainty some reference to diversity will be made during the interview. Try to relax and just be yourself answering questions with some detail, but try not to waffle. There are no questions to try to trip you up, but the questions are to explore your experience, attitudes and the type of person you are. This is why it is so important to, "just be plain you". You may get asked questions that refer back to your original competency questions on your application form or other things that you put down on your application form such as hobbies or interests, military service, current position. Results from various tests may also be looked at in more depth to probe your strengths and weaknesses. Being nervous is quite normal, however, try not to show you are nervous in the interview. The better prepared you are and more examples you give, the greater your confidence will be, once you have answered a couple of questions correctly. The interview panel will do their best to put you at ease. They are not there to fail you merely check you are the right kind of person and suitable for the role/force.
Remember questions around customer service, teamwork, and diversity are common questions, so think of examples that you could use. As this is what most people find difficult at competency based interviews – coming up with a good example. Keep talking until you have finished, fully and wait for any further questions. If they aren't any you have more than likely covered the question fully and will move onto the next question. Also enjoy the experience, this may well be the last hurdle before being accepted, so focus on the end being in sight, at the same time ensuring you do your best.

In summary, as I said at the beginning of the book, preparation is vital to give you the best chance possible, prepare and be in no rush, the more time you have in between each stage, the more time you have to prepare. Identify your weaknesses and see if they could hamper your chances of success, if so then work on them. Improve or maintain your fitness and work on your mental agility. As all will help during the recruitment process. If you don't succeed, find out or work out what you did wrong and improve on it before applying again. Many, myself included have had to apply at least twice to make it through a difficult and competitive recruitment process. The same can be said of both the PCSO and Special Constable Recruitment process. Most importantly - GOOD LUCK!!

### *Example PIRT/Psychometric tests*

### *Verbal Usage Test (Not part of PCSO or Police Officer Recruitment)*

1. One hundred officers ________ allocated for ____________ control.

A - was / croud

B - was / crowd

C - were / croud

D - were / crowd

E - none of these

2. It is _______________ to bring your uniform to the training _________.

A - necesary / centre

B - necessary / centre

C - necessary / center

D - necessery / centre

E - none of these

Answers Verbal Reasoning

1=D

2=B

### *Checking information test (Not part of PCSO or Police Officer Recruitment)*

Look at the two lists below and check to see whether the information in List A has been correctly transferred to List B. If there is a mistake in column A, mark circle A on your answer sheet. If there is a mistake in column B, mark circle B on your answer sheet. If there is a mistake in column C, mark circle C on your answer sheet. If there is a mistake in column D, mark circle

D on your answer sheet. If there are no errors in that line, mark circle E on your answer sheet. Note that there may be more than one error in a line.

LIST A

| A Date | B Name | C Time | D Ref Num |
|---|---|---|---|
| 12.1 | Williams | 13.30 | 2613 |
| 3.8 | Chan | 07.29 | 5971 |

LIST B

| A Date | B Name | C Time | D Ref Num |
|---|---|---|---|
| Jan 12 | WILLIAMS | 15:30 | 3612 |
| March 8 | CHAN | 09:27 | 579 |

Answers Checking Information

1=DE

2=CE

### *Practice Maths Test 1*

At the assessment centre, this is completed with a supplied calculator. You need to know how to work out, percentages, ratios, averages, area, speed, time and distance. Try these questions without and then with a calculator. Work through the easy questions then go back and complete the harder ones.

1. How much will five tins of soup cost at 55p a tin?

| A | B | C | D | E |
|---|---|---|---|---|
| £2.25 | £2.55 | £2.60 | £2.75 | £2.95 |

2. A person saves £35 in four weeks. At this rate how much will have been saved in one year?

| A | B | C | D | E |
|---|---|---|---|---|
| £200 | £250 | £355 | £420 | £455 |

3. What is the total cost of a journey when £1.65 is spent on bus-fares and an Underground ticket costs £2.50?

| A | B | C | D | E |
|---|---|---|---|---|
| £3.15 | £3.60 | £3.95 | £4.05 | £4.15 |

4. What is the average number of people per car, when six cars carry thirty people?

| A | B | C | D | E |
|---|---|---|---|---|
| 4.5 | 5.0 | 5.5 | 6.0 | 6.5 |

5. If shopping items cost £12.64, how much money remains out of £20?

| A | B | C | D | E |
|---|---|---|---|---|
| £6.36 | £6.63 | £7.36 | £7.46 | £7.63 |

Answers working with numbers

1=D

2=E

3=E

4=B

5=C

### *Practice Maths Test 2*

1) A grocer has sold £429 worth of fruit and vegetables. If there are cheques for £23.70, £50.35 and £26.95 and the rest is paid in cash, how much cash should there be?

a) £328

b) £101

c) £302.50

d) £428

e) £352

2) On average 1 out of every 25 shops owners experience violent assault. Out of 300 shops how many shops owners are violently assaulted?

a) 3

b) 4

c) 6

d) 8

e) 12

3) How much money remains if I have £55 and spend £23.75?
a) £30.75
b) £31.25
c) £32.50
d) £33.75
e) £33.15

4) You are allowed 22 days holiday, and have already taken 10 whole days leave and 6 half days leave, how many days holiday do you have remaining?
a) 8
b) 8.5
c) 9
d) 9.5
e) 10

5) You withdraw 40% of your savings from an account which holds £800. How much remains in your account?
a) £380
b) £420
c) £440
d) £480
e) £490

6) £13.83 is spent on Christmas shopping. How much change would you get form £20.00
a) £5.63
b) £6.17
c) £6.47
d) £6.67

e) £4.37

7) An oil drum has a maximum capacity of 800 litres. If the barrel is 75% full how many litres are required to fill it to its maximum?
a) 200
b) 300
c) 400
d) 600
e) 800

8) Eight cakes cost £6.08, how much is the price of one cake?
a) 74p
b) 76p
c) 80p
d) 81p
e) 82p

9) If a car journey of 490 miles takes 7 hours, what is the average speed of the car?
a) 55 mph
b) 60 mph
c) 65 mph
d) 70 mph
e) 72 mph

10) What is the average (mean) height of a group rowers if two are 1.80m tall, three are 1.95m in height and one is 2.10m tall?
a) 1.96 m
b) 1.90 m
c) 1.95 m
d) 1.94 m
e) 1.92 m

11) One case containing 42 bottles of orange juice cost £6.30. How much will 5 bottles of juice cost?

a) 10p
b) 25p
c) 50p
d) 65p
e) 75p

12) One vehicle in 15 is stopped in a drink drive campaign by the Police. How many vehicles will have been stopped out of 225?

a) 11
b) 15
c) 13
d) 12
e) 14

13) One carpet tile measures 50cm by 50cm. How many tiles are required to cover a floor which measures 10m by 2m?

a) 40
b) 60
c) 80
d) 90
e) 100

14) What is the total weight of five parcels each 200g and six parcels each 7.5kg?

a) 37kg
b) 38kg
c) 39kg
d) 42kg

e) 46kg

15) You start a shift at 2:30pm and finish at 10:30pm, how many hours will you have worked in five days?

a) 30
b) 35
c) 40
d) 45
e) 60

16) 8 magazines contain 110 pages each. How many pages are there in total?

a) 440
b) 660
c) 800
d) 880
e) 900

17) If you buy a CD for £6.79, what change is due from £10.00?

a) 22p
b) 23p
c) £3.21
d) £3.32
e) £4.21

18) You walk daily for 30 minutes, how much time do I spend walking in 10 days?

a) 3.5 hours
b) 4 hours
c) 5 hours

d) 5.5 hours
e) 6 hours

19) If my weekly paper bill is £3.50 and the delivery charge 45p per week, how much do I have to pay over six weeks?
a) £23.70
b) £22.30
c) £21.70
d) £24.70
e) £23.20

20) What is the average weekly wage of a team of five people whose wages are £220, £340, £325, £315 and £240?
a) £220
b) £288
c) £300
d) £320
e) £324

21) If turf costs 2.50 per metre, how much will 45m cost?
a) £106.50
b) £112.50
c) £120
d) £124.50
e) £126

22) What is the average age of a group of children whose individual ages are 13yrs, 15yrs, 8yrs, 7yrs, 7yrs?
a) 11
b) 12
c) 15
d) 13

e) 10

23) A motorist is travelling at 60mph, how far will he have travelled in 24 minutes

a) 21
b) 22
c) 24
d) 25
e) 26

24) If you withdraw £440 from a cashpoint. You get half the money in £20 notes and the remainder in £10 notes. How many notes do you receive?

a) 33
b) 31
c) 28
d) 24
e) 22

25) How many pieces of string 1.25m can be cut from a ball which is 100m long?

a) 130
b) 125
c) 95
d) 90
e) 80

Answers to Questions
Question 1=a
Question 2=e
Question 3=b
Question 4=c

Question 5=d
Question 6=b
Question 7=a
Question 8=b
Question 9=d
Question 10=c
Question 11=e
Question 12=b
Question 13=c
Question 14=e
Question 15=c
Question 16=d
Question 17=c
Question 18=c
Question 19=a
Question 20=b
Question 21=b
Question 22=e
Question 23=c
Question 24=a
Question 25=e

### *Verbal/logical reasoning test*

Sometime on the night of 4th November, the Zanzibar Club was burnt to the ground. The Police are treating the fire as suspicious. The only facts known at this stage are:

- The club was insured for more than its real value.
- The club belonged to Jim Tuttle.
- David Braithwaite was known to dislike Jim Tuttle.
- Between 3rd November and 4th November, David Braithwaite was away from home on a business trip.
- There were no fatalities.

• A plan of the club was found in David Braithwaite's flat.
A = TRUE B = FALSE C = IMPOSSIBLE TO SAY
1. A member of Jim Tuttle's family died in the blaze.
A B C
2. If the insurance company pays out in full, Jim Tuttle stands to profit from the fire.
A B C
3. The flat where the plan was found is close to the club.
A B C
4. Jim Tuttle could have been at the club when the fire took place.
A B C
5. There are definite grounds to arrest David Braithwaite for arson.
A B C
Answers Verbal Reasoning
1=B
2=A
3=C
4=A
5=B

## *Northshire Scenario Information*

You will be sent a similar scenario before you attend the assessment centre. Everything that is in the supplied information pack is there for a reason, have a good working knowledge of it, especially the equality statement and centre rules. As there will be exercises that relate to elements of these.
Introduction
We are pleased that you are joining us The Northshire Centre. We will ensure that we support you and that you settle into your new job quickly. Please read this induction guide to help you understand the Northshire centre as it forms part of your

induction. The information is designed to help you understand the centre, rules and policies to help you undertake your role as a customer services officer.

Within this information you will find:

- Information about the centre
- Operations Department
- Customer Services Officer – main duties and responsibilities
- Proposal Document Template
- Equality Policy Statement
- Code of Conduct.

Information about the centre

Opening hours

The centre is open from 9am to 8pm Monday to Saturday and from 10am to 4pm on Sundays and bank holidays.

Access

We have a car park for 5200 vehicles and there are roads that link to the local motorway and main roads. There are regular bus services to the centre from many of the nearby towns and villages. The nearest train station is at Addington and buses run every 10 minutes between the railway station and the centre.

Wheelchair access

There are wide malls and wheelchair friendly entrances to all shops and stores. All facilities are easily accessible to everybody. There are 150 car parking spaces for people who have a disabled person's badge. Wheelchairs and motorised scooters are available for free from the main customer services desk.

Shops

There are 132 shops, including two large department stores. Many of these shops are high street chain stores, but there are also a number of smaller independent shops and services. The shopping area is spread over three floors.

Food

The food court is in the centre of the Northshire Centre in the Dome area of the ground floor. There is a variety food and drink vendors to suit many people's tastes. There is also a licensed bar.
No-smoking policy
In line with current legislation and for the safety and comfort of everyone smoking is not allowed, except in designated areas outside of the centre. Or outside the shopping centres boundaries.
Customer service desks
The main customer service desk is next to the food court. There are two other support desks in the centre. Our friendly customer services staff will help you with any problems.
Medical facilities
The medical centre is run by a registered nurse and other qualified first aiders and is next to the main customer services desk and food hall. You can use the medical centre when the centre is open. The registered nurse will be able to give you a consultation.
Customer services
The customer services team is made up of ten Customer Services Assistants and four Customer Services Officers, who all report directly to the Operations Manager. The Customer Services Assistants work at the four customer service desks, providing information and help to visitors and customers.
The Customer Services Officers are responsible for dealing with complaints and any serious problems from anywhere in the centre. They do not supervise staff, but they do work with managers, the operations department, staff and customers on all customer service issues. The main customer service desk is located next to the food hall. All four desks are open at the same times as the main centre.
Housekeeping

The housekeeping team is made up of 15 full-time and part-time cleaners. They are responsible for cleaning all the general areas of the centre. There are two duty housekeepers who supervise the housekeeping team.

Security

The security team is made up of 27 security guards and three security supervisors. They are responsible for keeping buildings and property secure and for protecting the security and the health and safety of customers and visitors within the centre. The number of security guards on duty at one time varies from eight to 20. The security team also monitors the CCTV cameras (there are eight at various places around the centre).

Police

There is a police station in the centre. It is open at the same times as the Northshire Centre, but it is a place where customers can contact the police. Two officers from the local police station, take it in turns to manage the police station. As well as their other duties, they patrol the areas around the centre. They support the security team and try to respond quickly and help staff.

Customer Services Officer

Main duties and responsibilities

Customer Services Officers work in the operations department and are managed by the Operations Manager.

Customer Services Officers' main duties and responsibilities are as follows:

• To make sure that customers and visitors receive the highest level of customer service

• To receive, investigate and deal with complaints from customers, visitors and
staff who are not happy with any services

• When necessary, to write accurate reports of incidents, events and suggest ways to deal with problems

• To give staff and customers advice about the centre's Equality Policy Statement and make sure staff and customers meet the conditions of the statement

• To help managers make sure there are safe working practices in place in the centre.

• To provide a range of customer services to customers and visitors to the centre, (as it says in our policies), including:

• dealing with any serious problems

• making announcements over the tannoy

• helping with lost property when asked to by Customer Services Assistants

• providing information services

• looking after lost children until they are collected by their parents or guardians

• working with managers, the operations department and customers on all customer services issues.

Equality Policy Statement

This policy applies to every member of staff within The Northshire Centre when dealing with colleagues and customers. It is the policy of The Northshire Centre that no member of staff or customer should be unlawfully discriminated against or harassed. Discrimination includes treating a person less favourably because of age, sex, sexual orientation, gender reassignment, race, religion or belief, disability, marriage and civil partnership, or pregnancy and maternity. Harassment includes any unwanted conduct (including words, behaviour or a combination of both) directed at a person on the basis of age, sex, sexual orientation, gender reassignment, religion or belief, race or disability and which has the purpose or effect of violating a person's dignity, or creating an intimidating, hostile, degrading, humiliating or offensive environment. The Westshire Centre will not tolerate discrimination or harassment of any kind and takes all necessary steps to eliminate discrimination, harassment, victimisation and any other conduct that is prohibited by law and to advance equality of opportunity. We regularly review and monitor all of our practices and procedures.

Any person who believes that a member of staff is discriminating against or harassing a colleague or customer should take action as quickly as possible. We recommend doing the following:

**a**) Ask the person to stop. (In some cases, people may not be aware of the effects of their behaviour.)

**b**) Discuss the problem with an appropriate person. If you are not sure about what to do, whether the behaviour could be classed as discrimination or harassment, or whether you should make a complaint, you can get advice from a Customer Services Officer or your manager.

**c**) Make a formal complaint. You can complain in writing to the Centre Manager. The Centre Manager will then investigate your complaint and take appropriate action.

Code of Conduct

To make sure The Northshire Centre provides a safe, friendly and enjoyable environment for everyone within the centre grounds, you must not:

- behave antisocially including swearing, shouting, blocking walkways or public areas, acting dangerously
- display notices or wear clothing that other people may find offensive
- run, climb on or misuse escalators
- sit on barriers, fences or railings
- use lifts inappropriately
- use scooters, rollerblades, rollerskates or skateboards
- cycle in any areas other than on roads and parking places
- smoke, except in designated areas outside the centre complex

• use fire escapes, except in an emergency
• use or leave shopping trolleys in non-designated areas
• bring animals or pets (except assistance dogs) into public areas
• sell goods, carry out surveys or interviews, hand out leaflets or busk without our permission
• drink alcohol except within licensed premises
• commit acts of damage or theft.

The Northshire Centre reserves the right to escort anyone found to not be abiding by this Code from the premises and to ban individuals from entering the centre in future. Where necessary, the police shall be called for assistance.

Now you have all the background information just like you would be given before the assessment centre, you can have ago at the role play and written exercises. Remember to relate back to the background information as required.

## *Role Play Examples*

Example 1

In this exercise you have two pages of preparatory information

• A memo from Pete Green, Operations Manager
• An email from Pete Green, Operations Manager

During this exercise you will meet Hickling

Memo

To: 'You' Customer Service Officer

From: P. Green, Operations Manager

Ref: C Smith Customer Service Officer

A member of staff Hickling has recently just contacted me. They indicated that they are not happy with the behaviour of C Smith, Customer Service Officer, who recently approached them regarding some comments they were making about a new

employee in the centre. I understand that having spoken to C Smith about the incident, they informed me that the employee is from a minority ethnic background.
Hickling also mentioned that they have some concerns regarding our recruitment and selection process. I have attached a recent email that was sent in relation to our recruitment and selection procedures. I have asked Hickling to come and meet you today because I have an urgent meeting to attend.
Please meet with Hickling and deal with the matter.

Regards
P Green

P Green
Operations Manager
Email
To: All Staff
From: Peter Green, Operations Manager
Ref: Employment Policy
I have recently advertised for several vacant Customer Service Officer posts in the Stamford Today. All adverts contain our Positive Action Statement, which is as follows:
"It is the policy of The Northshire Centre that no person shall be treated less or more favourable on the grounds of political opinion, gender, marital status, religion, race, sexual orientation or disability.
The centre particularly welcomes individuals and staff from these backgrounds, as they are currently under-represented in the centre."
I remind all staff that although the statement is featured in our adverts, it does not preclude any persons from applying. All applicants will be required to undertake the same recruitment

process, the same standards apply for all, and we will only select the most suitably skilled candidate for the role.

Many thanks

Paul Green

Paul Green

Operations Manager

You have 5 minutes to prepare a plan and 5 minutes to meet with Hickling and resolve the issue with the highest level of customer care.

Example 2

In this exercise you have two pages of preparatory information

• A memo from Pete Green, Operations Manager
• An email from A Davis, Customer

During this exercise you will meet Davis

Memo

To: 'You' Customer Service Officer

From: P. Green, Operations Manager

Ref: Wearing of hats in the centre

We have recently added to our centre rules that "The wearing of hats or helmets whilst in the centre is forbidden, however hats may still be worn if they are for religious or medical reasons. This is for the safety of all employees, customers and visitors to the centre and aids in CCTV identifications." Please use your discretion and be polite when challenging anyone over wearing a hat, if you have any issues please refer to a customer service officer or manager.

I have attached the email of complaint that was sent in Davis by I have asked Hickling to come and meet you today because I am unable to attend.

Please meet with Hickling and deal with the matter.

Regards

P Green

P Green
Operations Manager
Email
To: Peter Green, Operations Manager
From: A Davis
Ref: Complaint
On a recent visit to the Northshire centre I felt quite upset that I was asked to remove my hat when I blatantly I saw foreigners wearing a Burka and a Turban and they were not challenged. I suppose because they are not from this country they get better treatment. I want a full apology from the security guard and assurances these foreigners will be challenged next time.
Regards
A Davis

You have 5 minutes to prepare a plan and 5 minutes to meet with Davis and resolve the issue with the highest level of customer care.

### *Written Exercise Examples*

Example 1
You are the customer services officer for the Northshire shopping centre. Your manager has asked you to compile a report regarding a number of complaints they have received from shop owners who state that rowdy youths are intimidating shop owners at the centre which is having a detrimental effect on their business generally and more importantly, their takings. Visitor numbers at the centre are down 20% over the last 2 months. CCTV reports suggest that a gang of 6 youths have been going round the centre during daylight shopping hours, often approaching customers and harassing them for spare change.

The local newspaper has become aware of these incidents and they are sending a reporter along to interview your manager to see what the main problems are and what the centre intends to do about them. Your report should detail your main findings and also your recommendations as to how the situation can be resolved.

Example 2

Your manager has received a request from the local council Anti-Truancy Group who wish to patrol the Northshire centre in groups of 6 people for a five day period next month. During their request the Anti-Truancy Group has raised concerns that school children from the local area are congregating at the Northshire centre during school hours. CCTV cameras have confirmed these reports. Local police have also confirmed in a recent report that anti-social behaviour in the area of the retail centre has increased by 15% in the last four weeks alone.

You are to create a report for your manager that details your main findings and your recommendations to resolve the issues.

Example 3

As the customer services officer at the Northshire centre you are required to provide your manager with a written report based on the following information. Currently at the centre there are 3 unoccupied shops. A local charity would like to use one of the shops for a 3 month period free of charge in order to raise money for charity by selling second hand clothes and goods. Your manager has already conducted a survey of all shop owners and staff at the centre to see what they feel about the proposal and the results are as

follows:

- 15% of shop owners support the idea.
- 5% of shop owners do not have an opinion.
- 80% of shop owners are against the idea.

- 90% of staff at the centre support the idea.

You are to create a report detailing your main findings and recommendations based on the information provided.

# APPENDIX

## *Example of an Assessment Centre Feedback Report*

Here is a generic example of the type of report you will be sent after the assessment centre. For ease I have removed some of the narrative and the actual titles for each section will be the name of the role play or written exercise. This candidate scored a D at interview for working with others, but averaged a B overall, but that one D brought the overall score down for Working with Others to 57%. Showing the impact of a poor example for that competency in the structured interview. If that D was a C or even a B it would have been high sixties, early seventies for the overall score! Good example of having at least two examples for each of the four structured interview competencies, which you now know will be given in your pre-assessment material.
The percentage scores you were awarded in this assessment centre were:
Overall 61% (Overall is not an average of all the grades)
Working with Others 57%
Oral Communication 93%
Written Communication 67%
Automatic Fail (D grade in Working with Others) No
Competency Feedback

1. Decision Making

Gathers, verifies and assesses all appropriate and available information to gain an accurate understanding of situations. Considers a range of possible options before making clear, timely, justifiable decisions. Reviews decisions in the light of new information and changing circumstances. Balances risks, costs and benefits, thinking about the wider impact of decisions. Exercises discretion and applies professional judgement, ensuring actions and decisions are proportionate and in the public interest.

You achieved a score of 47% in this competency area.

2. Openness to Change

Positive about change, adapting rapidly to different ways of working and putting effort into making them work. Flexible and open to alternative approaches to solving problems. Finds better, more cost-effective ways to do things, making suggestions for change and putting forward ideas for improvement. Takes an innovative and creative approach to solving problems.
You achieved a score of 58% in this competency area.

3. Professionalism

Acts with integrity, in line with the values and ethical standards of the Police Service. Takes ownership for resolving problems, demonstrating courage and resilience in dealing with difficult and potentially volatile situations. Acts on own initiative to address issues, showing a strong work ethic and demonstrating extra effort when required. Upholds professional standards, acting honestly and ethically, and challenges unprofessional conduct or discriminatory behaviour. Asks for and acts on feedback, learning from experience and developing own professional skills and knowledge. Remains calm and professional under pressure, defusing conflict and being prepared to step forward and take control when required.
You achieved a score of 47% in this competency area.

4. Service Delivery

Understands the organisation's objectives and priorities, and how own work fits into these. Plans and organises tasks effectively, taking a structured and methodical approach to achieving outcomes. Manages multiple tasks effectively by thinking things through in advance, prioritising and managing time well. Focuses on the outcomes to be achieved, working quickly and accurately and seeking guidance when appropriate.

You achieved a score of 50% in this competency area.

5. Serving the Public

Demonstrates a real belief in public service, focusing on what matters to the public and will best serve their interests. Understands the expectations, changing needs and concerns of different communities, and strives to address them. Builds public confidence by talking with people in local communities to explore their viewpoints and break down barriers between them and the police. Understands the impact and benefits of policing for different communities, and identifies the best way to deliver services to them. Works in partnership with other agencies to deliver the best possible overall service to the public.
You achieved a score of 75% in this competency area.

6. Working With Others

Works co-operatively with others to get things done, willingly giving help and support to colleagues. Is approachable, developing positive working relationships. Explains things well, focusing on the key points and talking to people using language they understand. Listens carefully and asks questions to clarify understanding, expressing own views positively and constructively. Persuades people by stressing the benefits of a particular approach, keeps them informed of progress and manages their expectations. Is courteous, polite and considerate, showing empathy and compassion. Deals with people as individuals and addresses their specific needs and concerns. Treats people with respect and dignity, dealing with them fairly and without prejudice regardless of their background or circumstances.
You achieved a score of 57% in this competency area.

Exercise Feedback

Role Play 1

In this exercise you met xxxx, a customer of The Northshire Centre, who wished to meet a member of the centre's customer service team.
The competencies you were assessed on and the grades you were awarded in this exercise are shown below:
Professionalism B
Service Delivery C
Serving the Public B
Working With Others B
Oral Communication A
Role Play 2
In this exercise you met xxxx, a shop owner at The Northshire Centre, who wished to discuss an incident at their shop.
The competencies you were assessed on and the grades you were awarded in this exercise are shown below:
Decision Making D
Openness to Change B
Professionalism C
Working With Others B
Oral Communication A
Role Play 3
In this exercise you met xxxx, an employee at The Northshire Centre, who had been asked to attend a meeting.
The competencies you were assessed on and the grades you were awarded in this exercise are shown below:
Decision Making B
Professionalism B
Service Delivery B
Working With Others B
Oral Communication A
Role Play 4

In this exercise you met xxxx, an employee at The Northshire Centre, who had been asked to attend a meeting.
The competencies you were assessed on and the grades you were awarded in this exercise are shown below:
Decision Making B
Openness to Change C
Service Delivery D
Working With Others B
Oral Communication B
Written Exercise 1
In this exercise you were required to write a proposal document in response to problems at The Northshire Centre
The competencies you were assessed on and the grades you were awarded in this exercise are shown below:
Decision Making C
Openness to Change B
Serving the Public B
Working With Others B
Written Communication C
Witten Exercise 2
In this exercise you were required to write a proposal document in response to an incident at The Northshire Cenre.
The competencies you were assessed on and the grades you were awarded in this exercise are shown below:
Openness to Change B
Professionalism C
Serving the Public B
Working With Others B
Written Communication B
Structured Interview
Candidates must answer 4 questions over a 20 minute period.

The competencies you were assessed on and the grades you were awarded in this exercise are shown below:
Professionalism C
Service Delivery A
Serving the Public A
Working With Others D
Oral Communication A

Psychometric Tests
You completed two psychometric tests; Numerical Ability Test and Verbal Ability Test.
In the Numerical Ability Test (NAT) you were presented with numerical reasoning questions and were required to select the correct response from a choice of options. This contributed towards your grade for Decision Making.
In the Verbal Ability Test (VAT) you were presented with various scenarios and a number of statements. This contributes towards your grade for Written Communication.
The competencies you were assessed on and the grades you were awarded in the psychometric tests are shown below:
Decision Making B
Written Communication A
Exercise by Competency Matrix
Written Communication C B A
Oral CommunicationA A A B A
Decision Making D B B C B
Openness to Change B C B B
Professionalism C B B C C
Service Delivery C D B A
Serving the Public B B B A
Working With Others B B B B B B D

29421594R00070

Printed in Great Britain
by Amazon